Walking Away

Simon Armitage was born in West Yorkshire and is the current Professor of Poetry at the University of Oxford. He has published ten collections of poetry, and is the author of two novels as well as the bestselling memoir, *All Points North*. In 2010 he received the CBE for his services to poetry.

Further praise for *Walking Away*:

'Very entertaining . . . The self-deprecation with which Armitage recounts these events is a big part of the book's charm.' *Spectator*

'Frequently superb . . . It's the felt quality of this poet's prose that marks it out.' *TLS*

'Even if hiking isn't your thing, the hours spent in Armitage's company are every bit as pleasurable as his numerous fans will have hoped.' *The Lady*

SIMON ARMITAGE

Walking Away

*Further Travels with a Troubadour
on the South West Coast Path*

FABER & FABER

First published in 2015
by Faber & Faber Ltd
Bloomsbury House
74–77 Great Russell Street
London WC1B 3DA

This paperback edition first published in 2016

Typeset by Faber & Faber Ltd
Printed in the UK by CPI Group (UK) Ltd, Croydon, CR0 4YY

A CIP record for this book
is available from the British Library

ISBN 978–0–571–29836–5

2 4 6 8 10 9 7 5 3 1

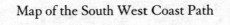

Map of the South West Coast Path

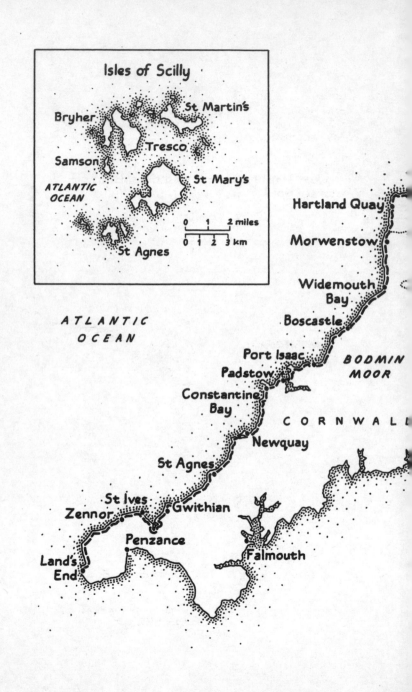

Isles of Scilly

Bryher
St Martin's
Tresco
Samson
St Mary's
ATLANTIC
OCEAN

0   1   2 miles
0 1 2 3 km

St Agnes

ATLANTIC
OCEAN

Hartland Quay
Morwenstow
Widemouth
Bay
Boscastle
Port Isaac
BODMIN
MOOR
Padstow
Constantine
Bay
CORNWALL
Newquay
St Agnes
St Ives
Zennor   Gwithian
Penzance
Land's   Falmouth
End

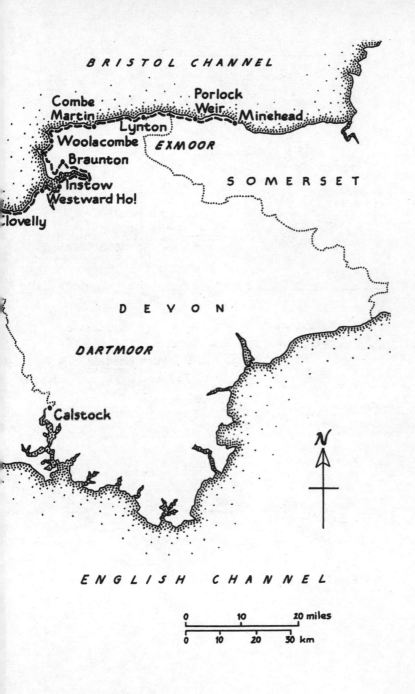

Introduction

In 2010 I walked the Pennine Way, and wrote a book called *Walking Home*. The conventional compass bearing for that particular journey is one of south to north, to keep the British weather out of the eyes and get a push from behind by the prevailing wind, and consequently all the guidebooks and most of the signposts point the hiker in that direction. But I walked south, from Kirk Yetholm on the top side of the Scottish border towards Edale in Derbyshire, a distance of 265 miles, a journey which would take me the best part of three weeks. The idea was to walk home, back towards the village of Marsden where I was born and grew up and which continues to be the focus for much of my writing, especially my poems. Being situated close to the southern end of the trail I used the gravitational pull of that place as a way of moving continually, if slowly, forward. The potential embarrassment of failing to arrive in my own postcode served as a further incentive to keep going, especially through the cloudier, boggier and more forlorn sections of the walk, of which there were many. As well as a challenge to my physical resolve and mental stamina, I conceived the walk as a test of my poetic reputation, giving readings every night in village halls, pubs, churches and private houses in return for board and lodging. Up until the early nineties I'd been a probation officer in Greater Manchester – how far had I come in that time? I took no money with me, and passed a sock around at the end of each evening, asking people to put in whatever they thought I was worth (which wasn't always currency, and it was with a certain amount of both curiosity and trepidation that I slid my hand into its lower reaches, never being too sure what my fingertips would discover). In fact in some ways I felt as if I was testing the reputation of poetry itself, wondering if an audience would turn out to hear spoken verse on a wet Wednesday in Wensleydale, and if there was a place in the contemporary world for a latter-day troubadour living on his wits and hawking his stanzas and stories from one remote community to the next. After the final audit, I declared a small financial surplus and an enormous emotional profit, though the demands of that journey on the body and the brain made me vow never to commit to such an undertaking again, because for all the beauty of the trail and the exhilaration of the experience, the Pennine Way is a brutal, punishing slog from start to finish.

Three years later, restlessness and imagination got the better of me. I convinced myself that my legs still had one last long-distance walk left in them, and started to think that *Walking Home* had only been half the project. If I really wanted to put myself on trial as a poet, rather than strolling around my home patch shouldn't I be striding out across the country in the opposite direction, getting further away with every step and spending time in places and with people as unfamiliar to me as I might be to them? After a few weeks of studying maps, totting up mileages and lining up cardinal points, I decided that a walk from Minehead in Somerset to Land's End in Cornwall offered a neat symmetrical opposite to the previous adventure. Specifically, the north coast of the South West Coast Path, a journey that by a quirk of maths is exactly the same distance as the Pennine Way. A walk this time not of boggy uplands, remote interiors, planted forests, unpopulated hillsides and uninhabitable moors, but a coastal journey, at sea level, in sunnier climes, through holiday destinations and tourist traps, towards accents and dialects different to mine and even into a separate language. Then rather than come to an abrupt halt at that far and famous corner of Britain, I'd overshoot, and go skimming across the sea to the Isles of Scilly. St Mary's, Tresco, Bryher, Samson . . . diminishing dots of land in the trailing ellipsis of the European archipelago, and the last opportunity for a public event in the UK before the vast, reader-less expanse of the Atlantic Ocean. Mystical Samson, whose population in the 2001 census is given by Wikipedia as '(1)'. I'd walk every day again, and read every night again, not stopping until I got to the end or the end got to me, but this time rather than walking home I'd be walking away.

Gearing Up

I have bought a hat. And I have made a stick. And both these objects say a great deal about the journey I think I'm about to embark upon. The hat was something of an impulse purchase, given that I don't really have a head for hats, and in recent years have been happy to suffer whatever complaints come with an uncovered crown rather than risk embarrassment or insult. I learnt the hard way: West Yorkshire wasn't ready for the peaked sailing cap I went for in the early eighties; neither did it appreciate my 'pork-pie' brown trilby during the ska revival era, and the ceremonial black bearskin I bought from a jumble sale one winter made me the worn rather than the wearer, as well as an easy target for snowballs. My wife looks good in a hat, any hat, and my daughter would look good even under a plant pot or lampshade. It's a certain face that suits a hat, or a certain smile, and I don't have either. My new hat, though, is no ordinary hat, as the dedicated display stand in Huddersfield Outdoor World and the price tag seemed to imply. For one thing, it's the only hat I've ever known that comes with an instruction manual, a four-page guide in small print with diagrams and specialist hat vocabulary explaining not just the practical aspects of hat ownership such as which way round it goes and how to put it on the head, but also the finer points of its design and functionality, as well as some conceptual issues relating to its philosophical significance in this world. Included within the terms of the guarantee is a lifetime insurance policy confirming that lost or damaged hats will be replaced by the supplier *at the drop of a hat*, as well as a strip of tear-off, pre-printed slips – the hat equivalent of the business card – to hand to admirers and enquirers, of which there will be hundreds. Almost unwittingly I seem to have bought into some kind of cult or owners' club, members of which include mounted police, guides and trackers, musterers and herders, field scientists, jungle explorers, extreme gardeners and military personnel from across all terrains and territories. As far as my own needs go, the hat's 50-plus UV protection factor promises to shield me against heatstroke, its three-hundred-and-sixty-degree brim will offer shade to my face and neck, and any perspiration will be absorbed by its built-in sweatband. It's washable, breathable and carbon neutral. It's made from a natural fibre which if not used by the hat manufacturer would have only ended up in an illegal cigarette and should help to ingratiate me with some of Devon and Cornwall's more alternative communities. It comes in an environmentally sensitive autumnal browny-green colour, ideal for blending in against a background of gorse slopes, seaweed-covered rocks and sandy coves. It boasts an inside pocket for money or plastic. Should the wind blow, the integrated bootlace can be looped under the chin and around the rear hemisphere of the head to prevent the hat blowing away over the edge of a precipice or across a beach, and there's no need to worry about it coming into contact with the sea because not only is it waterproof, it floats. And it's collapsible enough to make me the happy wanderer or easy-going rambler, but with just enough stiffness and body to distinguish me from the rank amateur and bumbling novice. All in all it seems like the essential head-wear for someone about to spend a month out of doors walking directly into the sun along the narrowing corridor of Britain's south-west peninsula at the tail end of summer. It will be my roof, my camouflage, my wallet and my begging bowl. But more than all that, when I stand in front of the vanity mirror in the shop with the hat on my head, rather than looking like a seventies Australian cricketer or a week-end ranger at a British safari park, I think I look sort of . . . normal. Sold.

The stick was also an impulse, though when I say I 'made it' most of the credit must go to nature itself and the organic processes by which a tiny seed is slowly transformed into solid timber. There's a dank and shady corner at the bottom of my garden, made danker and shadier by the handful of holly trees which grow there and the number of offspring they conceive every year. The shoots grow quickly and plentifully in the understorey around the trunks of the parent trees, and earlier this summer I was making the annual cull with a pair of rusty bolt-cutters and felled one particularly straight and surprisingly light sapling, whose circumference sat comfortably within my fingers and palm. I trimmed away a few twigs and sprigs, and the wood itself, once I'd shaved the slimy dark-green bark from the top five or six inches, was antler-coloured and bone-like in texture and shape, as if I'd stripped it of skin and flesh. I even considered whittling ornamental patterns or Celtic designs along its length but decided that might cast me in the role of an over-indigenous man of the hills or New Age rustic walking the spiritual highway of life with his shamanic wand. I left it outside through the big heat of June and July, through

Murray's Wimbledon and England's Ashes, imagining I was 'seasoning' it or subjecting it to a traditional and essential maturation process. The exposed 'handle' split a little, and the olive-toned cortex didn't weather or age as I thought it might, but by early August I considered that enough time had passed for it to have made the transition from lopped branch to walking stick, and it was coming with me.

The holly is a much mythologised and occasionally maligned tree, but both its reputation and its practical applications suit me very well. Holly is a hard, dense wood. It was once used for making the hammers in harpsichords and in the fashioning of billiard cues, and even though I'm not making a tour of concert halls and snooker clubs I like the idea of the stick as a totem of something rhythmical and melodic, accurate and true. As someone with an unreliable backbone, its rigidity and uprightness also appeal, as does its reputation as a tree which diverts thunderbolts away from houses and humans. Planted on paths and tracks, the tough evergreen acts as a way marker or beacon to the weary and lost, and in past times its branches and arms have proved useful as horse whips and batons. So the stick will be my signpost and my compass needle, and my cattle prod and my nettle slayer, my vaulting pole and my hatstand, and my extra leg and my spine. The holly is also symbolic of winter, and a charm against black magic and the dark arts. The berries, attractive as they appear, are bitter on the tongue and potentially poisonous. In those terms, I'm taking it with me as a piece of the Pennine north, out of season and out of place as I head into that long, low and increasingly treeless coastal region, a representation of who I am and where I'm from. Something of myself.

My dad, never one for getting hung up on the psycho-social significance of material objects but with a keen eye for a comparison, is able to offer an alternative interpretation as I climb out of his car at Wakefield Westgate with the hat on my head and my kit bag in my hand. In previous years that manoeuvre would have produced a waft of pipe smoke which would have followed me onto the platform and half-way to Birmingham. But since he quit there's no sign of the loose tobacco strands or spent matches that once clung to the seats and littered the footwell, no whiff of St Bruno Ready-Rubbed, and the ashtray is now full of small coins for the pay-and-display machine. A dedicated and expert smoker from early adolescence, his previous attempts to stop all ended in acrimony and deceit, and in one case farce, when on top of nicotine patches and nicotine gum and electronic cigarettes he was still secretly puffing on his pipe and had taken up cigars. This time, though, it looks like he's stopped for good, cold turkey following a worrying chest infection and the steep road between his favourite watering hole in the village and his house becoming 'a bit of a pull'. So today the only thing that trails me as I make my way towards the station entrance is the sound of a well-worn Duke Ellington cassette tape rattling through the car stereo. Sixty-five years of pipe smoke might have impaired his lung capacity – he could no more walk the South West Coast Path with me than he could run a marathon – but his ability to deliver a one-liner is undiminished. Through the open window he shouts, 'You've forgotten your staff, Moses.' I retrieve the stick from the boot of the silver Polo, then watch as he performs an illegal U-turn in the busy forecourt and heads for home, waving goodbye with the back of his hand.

Home to Minehead

Tuesday 27 August

Bishops Lydeard is everything we have come to expect from a station on a 'heritage' railway line: overenthusiastic staff in period uniform carrying handkerchief-size flags and buckets of water; milk churns converted to litter bins; wooden signage painted the colour of homely comestibles packaging (Ovaltine, Colman's Mustard, Lyle's Golden Syrup, etc.); destination markers in the shape of pointing fingers; rusting billboards advertising obsolete brands of cigarettes; and a cafe where a large urn hisses and gurgles at the end of the counter and where home-made iced buns are displayed on a cake stand and served on paper doilies. Everything bought

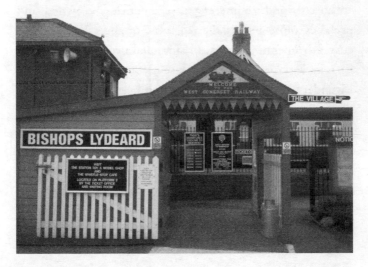

in the gift shop, even a 10p postcard, is handed over in a brown paper bag with an old-fashioned till receipt. The small bespectacled face in the booking-office window seems surprised when I ask for a single, even though the return is only a couple of quid extra. I tell him where I'm going, and he replies, 'Well, people have been known to come back from there.' When the train arrives, hooting hysterically and blurting out great plumes of pillowy white steam, I have a whole carriage to myself. It trundles along a single-track line cloistered by overhanging buddleia displaying semi-erect, vulgar purple flowers, then through dark and narrow cuttings, then out into open, rolling farmland with the Quantocks as a backdrop, slowing and halting at Stogumber, Williton and somewhere called Blue Anchor, where bearded porters stride purposefully alongside, blowing whistles and slamming doors. It wouldn't come as a surprise to pull into Adlestrop, or to see Bernard Cribbins on the platform checking his pocket watch. For a line run by enthusiasts and volunteers it's cleaner, less crowded and probably more punctual than most of the rail franchises currently operating across the national network. However, it's not a service you'd want to use if you were in a rush, and I wonder if it's a source of pride or embarrassment for locals that rail access to one of Somerset's principal towns is via a train offering packages such as 'Snowdrops and Steam' or the 'Santa Special'. Type 'Minehead' into the National Rail Enquiries website and the dreaded phrase 'By Bus' appears in the timetable. I pull my bags down from the luggage rack and head for the station exit. And there's no need to ask for directions – it's just a case of following everyone else out of the gates and along the prom, families mainly, some of them arguing with each other after a long journey, wheeling enormous suitcases towards the pinnacled white pavilion on the horizon.

*

The outward appearances are not encouraging. After guest check-in I'm directed towards a place called Strawberry Square in an area labelled Plantation Quay, which seems to be a series of apartments somewhere between Swiss chalet and mock-Tudor in design. The grassy strips separating each structure are scuffed and patchy. Varnish is peeling from the window frames of the buildings. The outside walls of each block are stencilled with large, unequivocal Soviet-style letters. Lots of men are wearing Premier League football shirts with their own surnames printed on the back. In a female voice, an uninterrupted stream of abuse and profanities issues from the open door of a ground-floor flat. Outside each block there's a rusty, Bronx-style fire escape, except it isn't an emergency exit but the exterior metal staircase leading to my second-storey accommodation.

Once across the threshold, though, it's a different vibe altogether, a spotless two-bedroom apartment (one double, one twin), all lemon-smelling and new-looking, with neutral colours on the walls and shiny appliances in the kitchen area. There's a flat-screen telly in the corner of the living room, shampoo in the shower, coffee in the cupboard and a framed photograph of a pebble over the headboard. On the bed there are two soft white flannels and a bath towel expertly folded into the shape of a kneeling elephant. It might not be home but I know I feel comfortable here because ten minutes later

I've taken off my watch, put it down on the chest of drawers, and I'm walking around in my bare feet.

*

This isn't my first time at Butlins. In the seventies we bought a family day-pass and spent seven or eight hours on the rides and in the swimming pool. I don't remember the location, possibly Pwllheli, though I can say with certainty that it wasn't the one in the Bahamas or the one in Mosney, Ireland, which underwent a relatively smooth architectural conversion from holiday destination to government-run centre for refugees and asylum seekers. But I do remember peering through the open door of one of the chalets as we walked past, which was more of a cabin or a manger, with a couple of beds in the room and not much else. And I remember the straggly barbed-wire fence that marked the perimeter, which my dad said wasn't to stop people getting in but to deter escapees. This was at a time when the sites were known as holiday 'camps', a word which brings with it all kinds of unfortunate imagery associated with incarceration or worse. Rebranding and refurbishment has sought to do away with all such connotations. Butlins is now a *resort*, and checkpoints and border crossings are also a thing of the past. Guests are free to come and go through the open gate, as are visitors and townspeople and anyone else with cash to spend. I wander around for a couple of hours through precincts and arcades, between chain-owned shops and outlets, from the Play Fort to Bob the Builder's Yard, then on to the Activity Gardens and Splash Waterworld, then into a 'residential' zone of 'streets' and 'lanes', among two-storey maisonettes, back-to-back terraces, detached bungalows, into Avocet Boulevard, Angelfish Park, Buccaneer's Way, Egret Villas, and transit from one neighbourhood to another without knowing if I've strolled into the posh end of town or onto the wrong side of the tracks. At one stage I find myself in the staff quarters, ranks of distinctly dilapidated barracks beyond the last supermarket, spookily quiet except for a tinny portable radio playing Capital FM next to an off-duty employee with a can of lager in one hand and a roll-up in the other, sunbathing on the pavement.

The dining options at Butlins are just as varied as the types of accommodation and no less stratified, but neither the heaving canteens nor the more exclusive restaurants have me on their lists. 'Are you a guest or a *guest*?' one doorman asks me using a combination of words and air-quotes. After rejection at several establishments I queue up at one of the fast-food counters, then navigate back to my own arrondissement, past kids yo-yoing from a high metal frame on elastic harnesses, past kids bouncing on a huge rubber diaphragm, past an adolescent Goth in full Dracula make-up and Hammer House regalia sulking outside a pub, past men in vests and three-quarter-length shorts, past young lads in gold necklaces and supernaturally white trainers, past young women in denim shorts and white stilettos, and grandparents pushing strollers or holding the hands of toddlers either screaming with excitement or inconsolably tired, and climb the clanging metal stairs and close the door.

*

I had tortured myself with the idea of giving a reading at Butlins, pitting myself against an eighties comedian, ex-

game-show host or army sweetheart, requesting a modest
venue towards the periphery of the encampment to see if
poetry could hold its own against the massed forces of light
entertainment. Or I'd wondered about trying to get a gig at
the Queen's Hall on the front, sandwiched between the
Strand Gift Shop and Merlin's Amusements. After all, poets
and the sea are natural companions, for proof of which look
no further than Watchet harbour just a few miles down the
road, where the agonised and emaciated form of Coleridge's
Ancient Mariner stands Christ-like on the harbour with the
dead albatross hung around his neck. Our earliest poems
were of the ocean – the Anglo-Saxon 'The Seafarer' and 'The
Wanderer' – and for well over a thousand years poets of every
generation and school have addressed the sea at some stage in
their writing life. But poets and the sea*side* seem a less comfortable fit, with the likes of Blackpool or Skegness promising
a sort of kiss-me-quick thrill that poetry struggles to supply.
I've given readings at hundreds of towns and cities across the
UK but rarely if ever on the coast itself, the one exception that
comes to mind being in Bridlington a few years ago, though
the actual venue was the orangery of Sewerby Hall, a former
stately home a few furlongs north of the slot machines and
the waltzer. (We used to go there as kids, even after an alpaca
had spat at my mum and my grandma had complained to the
zookeeper about a masturbating monkey.) It leads me to
wonder if the poetry reading is essentially an inland activity,
a notion I'm about to put to the test over the next three weeks.

Here at Butlins all that instant gratification and organ-
ised leisure takes place below the stretched tented roof that
dominates Minehead's skyline, a giant polytunnel under
which fun and enjoyment are hothoused and forced. So

instead of going head-to-head with *A Tribute to the Music of Ollie Murs* in a venue called Reds, or *Storytime with Billy Bear* in the Skyline Pavilion, I've taken a cowardly sidestep and opted for a more literary opening night, a metaphorical home fixture before the tour. I'm collected by Sandra, a local dispensing pharmacist who knows a thing or two about the non-public face of Minehead society but is too professionally discreet to go into detail. We drive east for about half an hour, past the fairy-tale structure of Dunster Castle, with the sea occasionally visible between stands of trees or at the bottom of a valley, then arrive via a narrow lane into Nether Stowey and pull up next to The Ancient Mariner public house, whose many advertised features include 'the largest car park in the area'. No. 35 Lime Street, the tidy-looking cream and olive property on the opposite side of the road, is locked, though eventually a face appears at the window and gestures towards an entrance round the back. This isn't my first visit to Coleridge Cottage. During the early nineties, after reading somewhere else in the county, I was invited by its custodian and resident, Derek Wolfe, to drop by the next day for a personal tour. In truth, there wasn't much to see or to link the house with one of Romanticism's presiding spirits and the place was pretty run down. But Derek was very excited because he'd been exploring in the attic and had discovered a wall which he thought might date back to Coleridge's tenancy. During the nineteen seventies it had been papered over with woodchip, but Derek was hopeful that beneath the modern decoration there might be an original wattle-and-daub partition, and even fantasised that Samuel Taylor himself might have scrawled something on it – a few words, perhaps, or even an undiscovered poem to rival his other great works of the period. We went upstairs with a cloth and a bucket of warm water, and after a few minutes of soaking and wetting Derek asked if I would do him the honour of peeling back the wallpaper. A long strip of it came away with a single pull, and below it, written in felt pen on a sheet of plasterboard, were the words 'Liverpool FC, Gods of Europe'.

Coleridge only lived here for three years but wrote some of his best and best-known poems during that stay. In the absence of any other residence or birthplace the cottage has become a geographical locus to at least counterbalance Wordsworth's Dove Cottage in Grasmere, if not to actually compete with it. Owned by the National Trust, the house underwent a major transformation in 2011 and has been cunningly retro-fitted to late-eighteenth-century standards. A 'resource' as much as a museum, visitors can now dress in period costume, look for pretend mice, sit at the very fire-place where 'Frost at Midnight' was penned, share in some of Sara Coleridge's domestic tasks or write with a quill pen, all under the glow of electrically powered oil lamps and plug-in candles. In the garden, a lawned path curves between pregnant apple trees and carefully chosen wildflowers towards the statue of a pig fashioned from willow rods, replacing the written-off car which languished there for several years. The view beyond is towards where the famous lime-tree bower was said to be located, now a neighbour's bungalow. After lemonade on the terrace, a bit of chit-chat with a few of the volunteers and accepting an invitation to gaze into a well, I read to a polite audience of thirty-five in the exhibition room at the rear of the main house. It's a fea-tureless, un-atmospheric space, but the National Trust's range of glosses and emulsions lend it a veneer of tradition, and it's quiet and calm, even with the door wide open. Birdsong fills the gaps between poems, followed by dusk. Afterwards a man asks me to add to his collection of autographs.

'Have you got many?'

'Not really. You're number four.'

'Who are the other three?'

'Little and Large and Geoff Capes.'

I leave the donations sock draped on the window ledge by the door. It's a saggy old knee-length thing in blue wool, and it lies there flat and deflated like a pathetic and somewhat pessimistic Christmas stocking, while I step outside into the twilight.

*

Suki from Vermont drives me back to camp. We follow the swell and dip of the trunk road along the coast, the lay-bys and verges lined with police vans and more sinister-looking unmarked vehicles, the woods and fields to either side harbouring sharp-shooters and marksmen, tonight being the first night of the government-sponsored badger cull and West Somerset one of the pilot areas. Through the trees I watch for the flicker of gunfire, or the iridescent flare of the high-vis jackets the hunt saboteurs are said to be wearing, or even the aura of frizzy silver curls around the head of celebrity protester Brian May, but it's just darkness followed by darkness, enclosing deeper darkness, until Minehead rounds the corner up ahead, the canopied roof of the giant Pleasure Dome throbbing with colour and light.

Minehead to . . . Minehead

Wednesday 28 August

I can't face a further interrogation or refusal by a Redcoat, so by 8.30 a.m. I'm eating breakfast in Morrison's cafe on the other side of the dual carriageway – surprisingly similar in tone and décor to Butlins itself. The very chatty woman on the till says she can tell what's on at the holiday resort by which products customers bring to the check-out. Lots of pasta, sausages and garlic bread during the school holidays. Hummus and muesli during the special Christian get-togethers. Rolling tobacco and Rizlas during the All Tomorrow's Parties music festival, and trolleys full of vodka and paracetamol on stag and hen weekenders. I'm not sure how she classifies me with my three brown rolls, slab of Gouda and a tub of Vaseline, but she helpfully points me towards a trading estate across the road in search of a phone charger, after which I wander into Minehead proper to sample the atmosphere and make a few uneducated observations about the place. The first of which concerns a road called The Avenue, which seems to function as an unspoken line of demarcation, with Butlins and all who visit there to the east and the town's more permanent residents to the west. Even further west, property values rise in direct correlation to altitude, where pretty lanes climb towards Higher Town under old pine trees and occasional flagpoles. Two towns, in effect, bisected by its main drag, sharing one bay and shoreline.

On the beach several people are already stripped down to their waists to catch some early rays, though they sit with their backs to the sea and their deckchairs facing the busy road along the front, because from a sunbathing point of view Minehead is the wrong way round. A bulldozer flattens sand under the promenade. The Avenue itself is a strip mall of knick-knack and fancy-goods shops, cafes, pubs, bookmakers, pound stores and tattoo parlours, plus the by now familiar sight of a closed-down bookshop, this one with a slurry of unopened letters on the other side of the glass door and just two books lying flat on one of the otherwise empty shelves: a paperback Everyman copy of *Moby Dick* and the 2012 *Top Gear Annual*. I stretch my legs along the criss-crossing paths that lead towards but never reach a place or thing called Beacon, telling myself that this lunchtime saunter and picnic in the woods counts as 'training', then head back to Butlins for a last mosey around the site. My stick I leave propped against the wall in the apartment lobby; as a lone, middle-aged man in a determinedly family environment I already feel self-conscious and conspicuous enough, and wandering around with a four-foot length of holly isn't going to help. Neither would I be confident offering the word 'poet' as an explanation. But with an ice cream in my fist and behind a pair of sunglasses I go completely unnoticed and unchallenged, and if truth be told, now the novelty has worn off I feel relatively comfortable here. In fact that's exactly what's so unsettling about Butlins – not the oddness or peculiarity of the place but its very normality, its ordinariness, the way that standing in the middle of its covered shopping precinct is like standing in the middle of Oldham or Basildon, with the same shops and cafes and bars to choose from and the same brands and products on sale. There's even a church. And a travel agent's, presumably selling more trips to Butlins, but who knows, maybe promoting weekend breaks in Rotherham or all-inclusive fortnights in Luton or Tamworth, because what Butlins offers is a home-from-home experience, a theme-park version of everyday life.

*

West Somerset College near the back of the town has its own public restaurant and therefore its own restaurant manager, or rather a Subject Leader for Hospitality, one Adrian Fleming, who used to teach English before a vacancy came along in the catering department which he stepped into and filled. One day he was teaching contemporary poetry, the next he was explaining the mysteries of a good risotto to Year 10 students embarking on a career in the south-west's all-important tourism industry. Such are the vagaries and flexibilities of the modern educational syllabus, I say to him, though I'm not sure if I offer the comment as congratulation or commiseration. No need to feel sorry for Adrian though because he's clearly in his element among the big aluminium pans and stainless-steel knives. Ruddy-cheeked from a recent walking holiday in the Swiss Alps and flushed from the effort of preparing spicy falafels and flatbreads for tonight's guests, he gives me a quick tour of the gleaming catering ovens and spotless fridges and introduces me to some of his star pupils – a would-be chef, an aspiring sommelier, a budding maître d' – before we sit down and discuss the format of the evening. Basically it's up to me, he says. I could go on after the sparkling-wine-set-with-agar-agar-served-in-a-champagne-glass starter or between the lamb kebabs and the dessert. 'I don't mind being the cheeseboard,' I hear myself saying. 'Fine with me,' says Adrian, who disappears into the kitchen to do something with a roll of tin foil. About forty people arrive for dinner and take their seats behind the precision-folded napkins and expertly laid cutlery. The PA system is a mic and box-amp arrangement with a timbre more readily associated with bingo calling or high-street busking, but it does the job, and an independent bookshop from Taunton who've set up a stall in the corner do a reasonable trade. The food is delicious and the service faultless. So faultless and so efficient in fact that by half nine we're heading home, back to Adrian's house through the college campus which merges seamlessly in the dark with the grounds of the local hospital. 'Very handy when students chop off their fingers with the meat hatchets,' he says. With his partner Becky we sit on low settees in his living room beneath the arching leaves of an out-of-control pot plant, flanked on one side by a bank of alphabetically arranged DVDs and on the other by a high wall of paperbacks ranging from serious non-fiction to popular fantasy. Adrian has what I think of as the classic chef's appearance: red face, shaved head and a bit of a cheeky grin. He says, 'I've cooked for Henley Regatta, the Hilton on Park Lane, the Ryder Cup, Peter Stringfellow, Thatcher . . .'

'What will your students be doing tomorrow?'

'Tonight's washing up,' he says.

'All part of the training, I guess.'

Adrian nods. 'Exactly. Some of them turn up thinking it's straight to the venison carpaccio on day one and look a bit despondent when I stick a tea towel in their hand.'

*

They're opening a bottle of wine when I head up to bed with a cup of tea. I'm in a back bedroom about the size and shape of the bedroom I had as a boy, which was actually an annexed section of my parents' bedroom, my older sister having sent me packing once we'd become too old for bunk beds. I think Adrian might have tidied up for me, might even have bought new bedding. Everything looks very crisp and fresh, not to mention very green, from the pale-green walls and curtains to the green patterns on the duvet cover and green sequins on the edge of the pillow case and the green LED numbers on the alarm clock. There's a shelving system cloaked by a dust sheet, with summer shoes stashed in pouches hanging from a rail, like insects in chrysalis, waiting to emerge. My stick leans against the door, its green, reptilian hide camouflaged against the green background, and a larger reptilian presence squats on the floor beside the bed. When I walked the Pennine Way an inordinately large suitcase travelled alongside me, sherpa'd by kind hosts and organisers who risked vehicle-suspension damage and a hiatus hernia as they lifted and lugged it from stage to stage, the case soon attracting the nickname The Tombstone. This time I've gone for something smaller in the same range, a Russian-doll version of its taller and wider relative, though having no less luggage the case is just as heavy, a squat and solid block of clothes and books, with every air bubble squeezed from its compacted layers. Lying flat on the carpet the stretched, overstuffed fabric of the lid forms a humped green dome, like the shell of one of those giant sea turtles bobbing around in the ocean or lumbering across a sandy beach, and with just enough phone signal to connect to Google Images I decide that the Galapagos tortoise, with its hemispherical carapace and five hundred pounds of body mass, is the most poetic comparison. I hear their voices underneath me, Adrian and Becky chatting and laughing, talking about grown-up things, and the sound of the telly, post-watershed, something with serious music and dramatic pauses. I'm sure I'm older than both of them but in other people's houses I seem to automatically assume the role of the child, the kid in bed surfing through galleries of animal exotica when I should be asleep with the light out. I've been away two days and two nights now and still haven't set off.

Minehead to Porlock Weir

Thursday 29 August

By 9.30 in the morning this is still the case, even though I've been walking for twenty minutes, because Adrian's house is a mile or so from the seafront. Also, as well as the rucksack and all the usual items of hiking paraphernalia, I'm carrying what is occasionally referred to as a 'food baby' in the form of a full English breakfast, a foetal agglomeration of pork, egg, beans and potato lying heavily in the bottom of my stomach which might even be twins. 'Do you want the works?' Adrian had asked me once I'd appeared in the kitchen, and seeing the rows of bacon and ranks of sausages already lined up in the grill pan there was only one answer. Pulling on his apron and clapping his hands together, Adrian fried and stirred while I ran my fingers across the books on the kitchen shelf, an eclectic selection of titles ranging from a handsome volume of Nigel Slater recipes to Bertrand Russell's *History of Western Philosophy*. After chowing through the meal we'd staggered onto the patio at the back for air and rest, and in a photograph taken by Becky the calorific heat haze and cholesterol-generated thermals eddying around our bodies are as good as visible. In that respect, a gentle stroll along the prom before walking in earnest is probably a sensible idea, and rather than grumble about the extra distance I choose to think of this as further training before the actual event, a turn around the paddock before getting out on the course.

The official starting post of the South West Coast Path is marked by Owen Cunningham's metal sculpture at the west end of the seafront, a large silver-grey fabrication which depicts two severed hands opening a folded map of the south-west peninsula, and just to ram the point home the words 'South West Coast Path National Trail' are written on the tarmac in white local-authority-font capitals, with a big acorn painted below and an arrow pointing out of town. Judging by the polished surface of the statue, the fleshy areas between thumbs and index fingers have obviously provided convenient places to lean or sit in the twelve years since it was first installed, and I duly spread myself against the cold metal while Tim takes a photograph and Adrian takes a breather in the form of a quick cigarette. I've known Tim for about twenty years but I didn't know his parents lived in Minehead or that he was a fellow member of the expensive-hat cult. He inflects a Masonic-like nod of approval in the direction of my head and no further words are necessary. As we set off we pass a camper van with a cardboard sign in the windscreen saying, 'Good luck, Simon, see you in Porlock.'

It's cloudy, with the tide out and a damp, warmish breeze blowing in off the sea. The mysterious uninhabited islands of Flat Holm and Steep Holm are visible in the Bristol Channel, though what I think is a third and therefore even more mysterious island turns out to be a moored oil tanker when magnified in Tim's binoculars. The low-lying coast-line of Wales comes and goes through the morning mist across a body of pewter-coloured, cold-looking water. The path leaves the old harbour and lifeboat station on the right and passes across a grassed dog-walking zone before enter-ing woods at the far side. What follows is a full-throttle ver-tical take-off, the track rocketing heavenwards in a straight line then zigzagging up through the trees, making the lilac and mauve boulders along the coast look like pebbles down below and bringing the blue and pink structures of Hinkley Point nuclear power station into view to the east, and fur-ther still, the iconic profile of Glastonbury Tor. The climb is too much for Adrian, who admits to being 'slightly off the pace' and waves us on, but not too much for Wanda, who has walked this stretch on many occasions and seems to have perfected a circular breathing technique allowing her to inhale and talk at the same time. Wanda initially appeared as a small dot about a quarter of a mile behind us with a loud voice shouting, 'Wait, wait,' in a Brummie accent. She arrived huffing and puffing behind a pair of steamed-up glasses and under a helmet of curly blonde hair, apologising for being late and reminding me that I turned down the offer of a night in her static caravan. Her face, now I can see her properly in the strengthening morning light, is stippled with little blisters and sores, as are her ears and the back of her neck, the result of being attacked by a swarm of horse-flies a few days ago, she says, something of an occupational hazard in these parts.

'Were you wearing insect repellent?'

'Yes, but they seemed drawn to it,' she says. 'And it's pro-nounced "Vanda". With a "V".'

'Caravanda!' I say.

But she hasn't heard. I walk behind her up the hill, my ears catching every second or third word of her life story, from her father's experiences in the coal mines of Silesia to her current work–life balance between a house in the Mid-lands and a campsite on the Somerset coast. After climbing through more oak and beech we break surface on a heath at the top of North Hill, in a landscape of charred and carbon-ated gorse, the ground underfoot scorched to dust and flak-ing ash, the weird dead branches and twigs like wiry blackened roots in the air. Half a dozen Exmoor ponies are standing around a bench at the edge of a car park waiting for biscuits and mints. For someone who's just been hiking in the shadow of the Matterhorn, Adrian appears distinctly unfit; by the time he catches up he looks like he might either expire or explode. And now he's gained this altitude there's no way he's going to squander it for the sake of a few plung-ing valleys and the smell of the sea. He'll stay on the tops and meet us in Bossington, he says, and sets off along the plateau, between the shrivelled ghosts of gorse bushes and past the yonderly, wind-ruffled horses. The 'rugged, alternative route' takes us along the shoulder of the coastline, with views

Minehead . . .

over the Channel broadening and sharpening all the time, then into my first 'combe', Grexy Combe, a perfectly symmetrical steep-sided V-shaped valley with a small stream in the bottom running directly for the coast, towards what looks like a dam wall built of variegated blues and whites and greys, which is the sea, topped by the clouds, topped by the sky. All decidedly non-Pennine in formation, and a reminder that this is new ground for me, a landscape and topography which is textbook British and peculiarly English, but foreign to these eyes and these feet. We watch a couple of peregrines gliding and dipping along the cliff edge, and a sparrow hawk jerking and scything towards a distant copse, then another peregrine which becomes invisible as it lands against a rocky backdrop. Then a raven – the first one I've ever seen beyond the walls of the Tower of London – like a battered old top hat, cronking and honking as it allows a convenient updraught to lift it out of the arms of a dead tree and put it down in a far field. In the trough of Henners Combe Tim spots a young red deer, then another two, so red it seems incomprehensible they could find anywhere to hide against the straw-coloured ground or the green bracken. But look away for a second then look again and they've merged into the pattern of the hillside, invisible to us now. It could be that they heard Wanda, who has put her spoken-word autobiography on hold while she enlightens us with snippets of information from her geology night class, starting in the Devonian period of the Palaeozoic era. Or maybe they were spooked by my ringtone, a phone call from a concerned friend who's seen online comments posted by the *Western Morning News*' Walking Correspondent suggesting that I've gone missing already. We ramble on through colonnades of mountain ash whose berries are so red and vibrant they look like fairy lights or hot, glowing cinders, then into unexpected clumps of oak and birch, bent and knotted trees often in a sheltered crook of the valley or cowering below a stony bluff or clinging to the lee side of the slope. Then through high bracken, along stony walkways and rust-red soil. On the steep descent of Hurlstone Combe a woman on a brown horse is coming towards us, its hoofs clattering and slipping in the fallen scree and loose shale, a brisk and busy Jack Russell nipping between the horse's legs as it trudges up the gradient. 'We call this the north face of the Eiger,' says the woman when we meet. I expect her to be sweating and exhausted, but of course it's the horse doing all the work. She's rather immaculate in a pair of spotless cream jodhpurs and with a neatly braided ponytail hanging down her back. Her black leather Harry Hall boots are so polished I can see my face in the toe end of one, which is about level with my chin. She tells us that her mount answers to the name of Amir and we agree to disagree about the reason chestnuts or 'night eyes' form on the inside of a horse's front legs, those leathery knobbles which are sometimes used as a form of identifying mark or 'fingerprint'. (A vestigial toe, I read later, is the best explanation for this kind of lump. Not the lesion where the animal was once joined to its mother's womb, as Amir's owner believed, and certainly not the result of its knees knocking together when it walks, as I'd suggested, though if I'd carried someone up the north face of the Eiger I'm sure I'd have calluses to compare.) We picnic on the prow of Hurlstone Point, next to the stone-built National Trust collection tin and a sturdy bench, which gives several flying bugs the opportunity of homing in on Wanda's anti-insect spray, Tim the chance to photograph a butterfly and me the challenge of finding a point of entry into one of Adrian's industrial-sized sandwiches, from a lunch box which also includes a complimentary Swissair chocolate. We hear music getting louder, the fizz and wash of compressed techno rhythms, and a few minutes later four young lads march past, the leader wearing a rucksack with two conical, metallic pink speakers like Madonna's bra tied to the front straps pumping out synthetic bass lines, electronic drumbeats and simple repeated patterns of high-frequency notes, like a child playing 'Chopsticks' in a tumble drier.

Bossington village looks like a picture postcard of thatched houses. Along one lane we bear witness to a biblical tableau of several large goats in an open-sided stall, all sporting impressive horns and tapering jazz-style beards. Bossington Beach, to where it becomes Porlock Beach, is a shingle ridge comprised of rolling, lead-coloured stones that form a natural barricade and sea defence, protecting the villages of Bossington, Porlock and Porlock Weir and the low-lying fields behind it from the marauding waves. But after years of repairing the bank to hold back the tide, and following major breaches in the nineties and a subsequent policy of managed retreat, what was once a freshwater pasture has become a saltwater marsh. The route picks its way across a complex maze of paths and pontoons, through the boggy fields, brackish ponds and sluggish channels of what is still a farmed and grazed vale but is destined at some point to become that darling of the geography field trip, a lagoon. The pelvis and spine of an aurochs was excavated from the ground here, close to the remains of a submerged forest, and once entered the area has an ethereal, forgotten feel to it, a lost or liminal space appearing and disappearing between weather and eras and tides. An atmosphere reinforced by spectral herons, by the upright silhouettes of dozens of dead trees protruding from the tarry soil – a bone-yard of skeletal branches and trunks bleached to a silvery-white by wind and salt – and by the veil of fine sketchy rain drawing in from the south, the perfect mood-music for this world within a world.

Wanda has veered off towards her immobile home and Adrian has used the descent from Exmoor to provide him with the necessary momentum to join us for the final slog along the shingle ridge to Porlock Weir. The dampness in the air – more of an overenthusiastic fog than actual rain, but drenching and cooling nonetheless – has transformed the colour of the stones to a chocolate brown, or so it seems in the fading afternoon, and they rattle and clatter like bro-ken crockery or heaps of clay pigeons as we crunch and scramble towards the harbour and the clutch of houses beyond the masts of four or five small boats.

*

What I mistake for Porlock Village Hall is actually the tour-ist information centre, but the woman behind the counter recognises me from the poster advertising tonight's reading and points me in the right direction, telling me the Arts Fes-tival has sold over a hundred tickets and are currently look-ing for more chairs. In the hall itself, just around the corner, there's a major panic because the lectern hasn't arrived. The man deputed with setting up the PA system asks me to per-form a soundcheck by telling him what I had for breakfast, and I'm only about a third of the way through this morning's extensive menu when he raises his hand and says, 'That'll do.' One of the organisers suggests I go across the road to the Ship Inn for a drink, an ale house dating back to the thirteenth century, and I sit in the beer garden with my notebook open and pen in hand. Poet Laureate Robert Southey was said to have knocked off a poem while leaning on the bar at the Ship, the sonnet 'Porlock', with its somewhat obsequious tone and complacent rhymes, leading me to wonder if he was after a free drink or even a room for the night. Not that I'm in a position to sneer at a poet who offers his work in return for bed and board, and in any case most poems are lucky to have the lifespan of a mayfly, let alone to still be fluttering their wings two centuries later. I stay in the pub for a couple of hours and leave with a lighter pocket, an empty page and a half-formed 'set list' in my mind.

Porlock Village Hall feels like two village halls with a connecting passageway, a catamaran of a village hall, as it were, with tea and wine being served in the port hull and the audience taking their seats to the starboard. I begin by explaining why I'm here and where I'm heading, and as a way of saying something about where I've come from try out a new poem called 'Privet', about the garden hedge at the house where I grew up, a dividing line with civilisation and cultivation on one side and bleak moorland on the other, a final boundary before the treeless and windswept hills that rose above the village. The hedge was planted when the house was built, in the early thirties, and must have rooted in fertile earth, reaching ten feet high in places and always in need of a haircut, especially during the long hot summer holidays of my childhood. Misdemeanours in the Armitage household were punishable by chores, a fair system, I now see, combining both retribution and reparation. One such chore was to trim the hedge, a double punishment since it necessitated an expedition down the cellar stairs, to the dark and clammy dungeon of the 'coal place' to retrieve a pair of shears which hung like Christ crucified from two nails driven between bricks in the wall. The shears were ancient, rusty and reluctant, not to mention heavy and blunt, and hacking through the overgrown mass of branches and leaves would take a puny ten-year-old most of the day. One evening, when I'd finished chopping and cropping and stood ankle deep in cuttings, my dad came out of the back door with his pipe in his mouth and his hands in his pockets and walked the length of the shorn hedge, inspecting the work, running his eye along the sides and the crown. Then, without warning or explanation, he lifted me up in his arms and laid me down on top of the hedge and left me there, floating on a bed of stalks, held up by nothing but twigs, staring at the sky.

I'm staying with John and Linda, retired civil servants who help run the Arts Festival, in their self-contained guest suite on the top floor of their house, which looks like a bungalow from the outside but feels several storeys high once I've hauled the Galapagos Tortoise into the attic. A Velux window looks west, roughly speaking, over neighbouring rooftops, over the de-horned spire of St Dubricius Church, across the cricket club and towards Porlock Hill. There's a primary school down there somewhere, in the valley bottom, which isn't unusual in a place of 1,400 people, except that Porlock has a reputation as the most elderly community in Britain, with over 40 per cent of its residents identified as being of a pensionable age at the last census. The bowling green sees more action than the football field, I imagine. There's no gas supply here, a wobbly phone signal, wavering internet access, one main road in and out, and an air of privacy or seclusion, which on another day could be interpreted as isolation and remoteness given the ambushing wall of high moor to the rear and the triple barrier of marsh, shingle ridge and sea to the front. As night falls there's no light pollution, just a glitter of uncountable stars in a sky that gets deeper and denser over a village which is finally blotted out by the rich, thick blackness outside. I go to sleep with the window open, and wake several times when I sneeze or roll over and an oversensitive motion-controlled bedside lamp comes alive and glares at me with its dazzling, interrogation-strength bulb.

Porlock Weir to Lynton

12.5 MILES

Friday 30 August

At Porlock Weir someone leans out of an upstairs window of the Bottom Ship Inn and shouts, 'Morning, Gandhi,' then disappears. Annie and Chris, landscape architects and complete strangers, are waiting for me in the car park, but first I have an appointment with a dame. Margaret Drabble, aka Lady Holroyd, was at the reading last night and has invited me for coffee at her house behind the harbour, but not before half past eight or she'll still be in the bath. I unlash my boots in the porch, even though she insists I can keep them on, and follow her through to the front room. She's just ploughed through an entire novel looking for a single quote but hasn't found it, which leads her to say that the electronic book might mean the death of the publishing industry but the word-search function is a life-saver, and has also reinvigorated long car journeys in the Drabble family with games like Guess How Many Times Shakespeare Used the Word Ocelot, for example. I can just about make out the odd Yorkshire vowel in her inquisitive conversation, and something perhaps of a Yorkshire manner in the directness of her questions and her interpretation of the answers. In a very British way I wouldn't dream of mentioning the rumours of a feud with her sister about the literary rights to a family tea set, but feel easy enough in her company to enquire how she once harboured one of the world's most wanted men. Putting a comic slant on the story she says that when she politely offered Salman Rushdie sanctuary here at Porlock Weir she never imagined for a moment that he'd accept, let alone turn up with several members of Special Branch and take over the entire house, which she'd only just finished renovating. We look out of the window and talk about the view across the Channel, how Wales sometimes looks like a distant continent yet on other days appears to be just a short swim away, depending on the weather. Before I leave she tells me that she'd gone out without her purse last night and now insists on putting a fiver in my hat, slightly awkward since I happen to be wearing it, but touching and gratifying, and ironic in the sense that the first and only other time we met was twenty-five years ago, when she handed me a cheque for what felt like a small fortune for a bunch of poems I'd written when I should have been studying social policy and reading Haralambos and Holborn rather than Homer and Hughes. I was a trainee probation officer at the time and splurged the whole lot on a flame-red Ford Fiesta and a corduroy jacket. Margaret Drabble says, 'I'm sure it was money well spent.'

*

Annie and Chris are friends of a friend, I discover, as we set off up the treed incline out of Porlock Weir, under ornate stone arches, on a leg of the journey described as 'challenging' in the guidebook due to the distance, the terrain and the fact that there's no settlement to speak of between here and Lynton, not even a cafe. And any lingering illusions about the South West Coast Path being a paddle along the strandline will be dispensed with once and for all today; most of yesterday's journey was spent well away from the water, both in terms of height and distance, and much of today will go by at greater altitudes, even further inland, often behind hedges or under woodland canopy. Holm oak, hazel and sweet chestnut form a guard of honour along the first three or four hundred yards, and after half an hour under the dark-green shade, among the twisted trunks and exposed roots, it feels like we're heading deep into one of those enchanted forests of book or film, where a faun might be suddenly glimpsed in a glade or dell, playing his flute, or a herd of satyrs seen cantering through the shadows. There are overgrown terraces here in the grounds of the ruined Ashley Combe House, and the remnants of wayside shrines and grottos, and intricately crafted walls studded with flint or pebbles and edged with slate. There are tunnels as well, said to have been constructed so that Countess Lovelace, Lord Byron's daughter, could look out across the gardens and ocean without the sight of labourers and minions inter-rupting the view, and I think we can all imagine how tire-some that would have been. Passing between two holly trees I half expect my stick to quiver with some kind of familial recognition – it's that kind of place – and at a turn in the path someone has constructed a mini Stonehenge from rocks and pine cones, albeit it to Spinal Tap dimensions. One construction whose sacred and mystical credentials are not in doubt, however, is Culbone Church, sometimes described as the smallest church in England and certainly one of its oldest. St Bueno's, which merits a place in the Domesday Book, stands on a site that might well have been a place of worship since the Bronze Age, and wears as its

spire the missing pinnacle from Porlock Church, which was carried here by a giant. A congregation of thirty people constitutes a full house at Culbone, though parishioners have to be pretty determined to attend services because there's no road other than the dirt track which brings us towards what appears to be Culbone's very own scale model, or a house made of gingerbread. In the graveyard a high and austere stone cross extends upwards from a circular plinth, and the gravestones, many of them commemorating family members with the surname Red, look like yachts in a storm, pitched and tossed, standing at all kinds of angles and alignments. In fact the whole church appears to lean forward, looming above the porch and the wooden door, which we stoop beneath to enter its cold, simple interior. Like most churches it feels like a space set aside, an enclosed otherness, but there's none of the usual echo and none of the intensified, reverberating silence often found among the outlandish heights and depths and breadths of religious architecture, just proportions and perspectives on a humble, human scale, so that in this particular house of God, God would probably take the form of someone very much like ourselves. Pharmacist Sandra, who drove me to Nether Stowey, told me that she walked here one day with her daughter and waited politely outside while what sounded like a carol service or choir practice took place behind the closed door. Eventually the music stopped and they went in, only to find a completely empty building. The rows of wooden pews have been buffed and reshaped by seated bums and bony spines, just as the flagstones and handrails testify to a long history of shuffling feet and sweaty palms. But there are signs of recent activity too, like fresh flowers on the altar. And modern trappings, such as the Calor Gas light masquerading as a candle in a glass lantern, and the small fire extinguisher, and a red fire bucket full of sand into which someone has thoughtfully stubbed a cigarette. A framed placard reads, 'For nearly a thousand years, as shepherds put their mark on their lambs, so the children of the Good Shepherd have been baptised at this font.' A list of rectors hangs on the wall, which if the legends are to be believed should go as far back as Joseph of Arimathea. I lift the lid of the harmonium and play 'Oh Will You Wash My Father's Shirt?', then sign the visitors' book and close the door, as instructed, to keep out the swallows. Back inside I hear the heavy metal hasp fall into its keep with a satisfying clunk.

Ash Farm, directly south of here, might have been the site of one of poetry's most enigmatic and anecdotal encounters. Waking there from a vivid dream one morning in 1797, Coleridge picked up his quill to transcribe the poem 'Kubla

Khan', which had come to him word for word during his sleep. But his trance-like concentration was broken when he was 'called out by a person on business from Porlock and detained by him above an hour, and on his return to his room, found, to his no small surprise and mortification, that though he still retained some vague and dim recollection of the general purport of the vision, yet, with the exception of some eight or ten scattered lines and images, all the rest had passed away like the images on the surface of a stream into which a stone has been cast'. So the dazzling, bewildering, incantatory poem usually referred to as 'Xanadu' remained incomplete. Today Ash Farm goes undisturbed, by me at least, since the path veers north towards the shore, along a lane so upholstered with spongy, luminous green moss it has the appearance of a sea bed or coral reef. Then twists due west along a bridleway and through cattle fields, the lower route by the coast being closed due to subsidence and land-slip. At Silcombe Farm, I watch one old boy raking grass cuttings from a forty-five-degree lawn, and another strug-gling back up the slope with a monster beetroot in his hand, like a severed head carried by its hair. It's a muggy morning; the cooked breakfast of two days ago still feels as if it's being extruded through my sweat glands and pores, and it's refreshing in every way when the vegetation parts or a vista opens up across a mown meadow or through a gateway to let breeze and brightness come sweeping in from across the sea. Then it's back into a narrow channel between two high hedges of oak apple, beech and blackberry, all knitted and knotted together, with occasional foxgloves spearing through the tangle, shaking their purple bells and cups, alongside desiccated versions of the same flower like spent rockets or flares. Then along a drive with wild-boar gargoyles above the gateposts, then through miles of rampant rhododendron, high enough to make the path a tunnel at times, the trunks and branches beneath the leaves impenetrably dark and endlessly interlocked. Nothing grows beneath this stuff. Above a steep waterfall, in an attempt to control the proliferation, some brutal act of botanical cleansing has taken place, and evidence of the cull lies jumbled and junked, ugly mounds waiting to rot away or roll into the sea. But the rhododendron has spread for miles in every direction, and there are signs of recrudescence even among the hacked limbs and scorched earth, a vigorousness that looks as if it's here to stay. And as ugly as the species is in such profusion, the wall of blue and pink petals must be beautiful from the water when this stretch of the coast is in full flower, and surely visible from the coast of Wales. Chris stops every once in a while to identify a bird by its song, and on one or two occasions whistles back to a redpoll, linnet or spotted flycatcher in its own tongue. After plantations and 'pinetums', and after crossing unceremoniously into Devon, open ground eventually arrives on the exposed heath leading to Foreland Point. The rolling banks on both sides of the valley are a mass of gorse thrones and footstools of heather, their golds and purples threaded and stitched together, then we round Butter Hill, with the protuberance of Lynmouth Beach visible down in the bay and the great mirror of the sea like a moving map of late-afternoon sky. The descent is a long slow traipse which includes the bloody impertinence of ten yards of road and not even a pavement. Following the relative isolation of the day it's peculiar to be parachuted into a world of ice cream and postcards, to be hiking past tourists who have arrived here by road and are experiencing the seaside by driving as close to it as possible, then staring at it through the windscreen. Annie and Chris go one way and I go another, across a pretty white bridge spanning a narrow, muddy channel. It's hard to equate the apologetic trickle of water down below with the deluge of rain, trees and boulders that burst through the town sixty years ago, flooding, destroying and killing. The official path actually zigzags all the way up the slope behind the seafront, but after almost thirteen miles I'm in no mood for its pedantic ascent so buy a ticket for the 'railway', an eccentric, ingenious and almost vertical contraption that forms an umbilical link with the higher community

of Lynton and is powered entirely by water. The tracks look like a pair of ladders propped against the hillside. So with the ring of a bell and the flush of a chain about a dozen of us are yanked upwards by the weight of a similar number of passengers plus a critical mass of H_2O in an identical carriage on a parallel line heading in the opposite direction.

*

B&Bs are not what they used to be. Southcliffe might have a foreboding appearance, but behind the pointy hat of its gothic turret and the dark wooden bedroom doors it's pretty much 'boutique', with furry cushions on the bed, a leather reading chair, a TV on the wall and products in the shower extending well beyond shampoo and soap to lotions and balms at the more esoteric end of the range. Sue wears flip-flops and a ring on her toe. I warn her against touching my boots, which are radiating heat and odour on a mat by the door, but she picks them up with her bare hands and takes them round the back to be housed in a decontamination unit or to be kennelled for the night. Andy is wearing something diagonal on his upper half, like a tae kwon do outfit or a shirt that Kraftwerk might wear in concert, which I realise after a while is his chef's top. They're runners and walkers and came here from Sussex for the environment and quality of life as much as anything else. Managing a guest house is hard work, but they've modernised and adapted to meet the high expectations and exacting demands of the contemporary tourist, and the number of repeat visitors to Southcliffe every year tells them they're doing something right. Queenie, a Bedlington–lurcher cross, isn't theirs, she's just on a sleepover, and after dinner waits in the lobby in a sequinned pink neckerchief, which in dog world is the de rigueur apparel for an evening of poetry. I read in Barbrook Village Hall, a couple of miles upstream on the West Lyn river, to an audience of forty-three people dominated by two strapping farmers, one of them the owner of Ash Farm. I'm almost certainly the hottest ticket in town tonight, though admittedly the petrol station across the road is still open and is selling half-price geraniums in the forecourt. On a big soft cushion on a large wooden seat next to an anglepoise lamp I could be presenting an episode of *Jacka-nory*. After the reading I tell Sandra's creepy story about Culbone Church and a man says, 'Ah, there's somebody here who can solve that mystery.' I'm escorted into the little kitchen at the side of the hall to meet a small woman at the sink in an orange cardigan and yellow rubber gloves who dunks crockery into a bowl of soapy water while listening to the tale and nodding at the details. There's a moment's silence once I've finished, before she offers the explanation.

'It was a ghost,' she says.

Then she carries on stacking saucers in the drying rack.

*

Not long before midnight a pair of headlights illuminate the drive of Southcliffe B&B. It's my wife, an unscheduled visit and something of a mercy dash, one of those occasions when it feels better to be together than alone, given the news and the mood. About twelve hours earlier I'd been slipping and sliding down a combe under Sugarloaf Hill when a journalist from the BBC rang, wondering if I'd give a quote about Seamus Heaney, and when I asked why, she said, 'Oh, I'm sorry if you hadn't heard. He died this morning.' For most of the afternoon I'd been spluttering lament and eulogy into the phone until I didn't want to talk any more, just turn poems and lines over in my mind, and let my memory drift from the poems to the poet, to recollections of the person himself. Like picking him up from a Bristol hotel one morning and asking him if he'd had breakfast. 'No, but I've got this,' he said, holding up a peppermint Aero bar, making me wonder if the bubbles in the chocolate were the key to poetic brilliance. And boozing all afternoon with him and Bernard McCabe in a ramshackle pub under Clee Hill in Shropshire, then later that night in Bernard's garden outside Ludlow, still opening bottles, when Bernard asked him if he'd written his talk on Housman for the Festival lecture the next day. Seamus said he hadn't and probably ought to scribble a few notes before it got light, and when Bernard told him there was a little writing table in the bedroom where the Heaneys were sleeping, he said, 'Ach, don't bother. I'll write it over the wife's rump.' And at a reading at London's South Bank Centre a year ago, when he didn't have the energy to walk across the complex to write and sign a poem in a global anthology called *The World Record*, so pen and book were brought to him, and the table as well, carried along corridors and up staircases, causing him to blush at the embarrassing palaver of it all, then to hang his jacket on the back of the chair and settle to the task in his braces and shirtsleeves. And in a cafe in Dublin, which must have been a regular haunt, because they gave him a quiet corner near the back, away from the windows. I asked him if it was a strain, being noticed and approached all the time.

He replied by saying that a few days ago he'd been walking past a bar where a couple of lads were out on the street having a smoke, and after he'd gone by he heard one say to the other, 'That's yer man.' The kind of affirmation that appealed to him greatly, I think: unsought, unobtrusive and from street level, despite him being one of the most decorated and recognised writers the world over, and in many ways the ambassadorial face of post-war poetry. That common touch was his genius, because in his work and his manner he could speak to both the tenured professors and the general public with the same sentence, in the same breath. A chieftain among poets, a scholar among critics, and among readers a citizen of the world. And an ever-present on the poetic landscape from as far back as I can remember, but now gone. In the dark of the bedroom, on the glowing screen of a mobile phone, we read 'Blackberry Picking', and we read 'Death of a Naturalist' and we read 'The Forge'.

Lynton to Combe Martin

Saturday 31 August

Andy and Sue are my new best friends, so I put my arms around their shoulders and we have our photograph taken outside the guest house before I set off through Lynton with the other Sue, my Sue, the roads empty and the town still sleepy and quiet. The few people we do meet are looking for me, so by the time I get back on the trail proper the passenger manifest reads as follows: Rob, a former bookseller who now runs an online wooden toy company; John, a maths teacher from Norwich who has arrived in the southwest on his bicycle; Carolynn, organiser of last night's reading and sometime keyboard player in a local jazz band; Roland, who I think might be Carolynn's husband or partner; and a man called Keith who has recently undergone spinal surgery, who falls behind almost immediately and is never seen again. Today's section is long and 'challenging', and in its final reaches will take in Great Hangman, the highest point on the whole of the South West Coast Path. But before jumping to too many conclusions about the journey ahead it's always worth looking at what the locals are wearing, which in Carolynn's case is a pair of sandals, making me optimistic about both the terrain and the weather. The route out of Lynton is along a tarmacked path, smooth and flat, which cambers between outcrops and along the cliff face before heading into the very peculiar Valley of

Rocks, a 'hanging valley' cradled parallel to the coast rather than opening towards it, with a stony 'castle' formation on the right and other enigmatic outcrops on the left with names such as Ragged Jack and Devil's Cheesewring. It's a Spaghetti Western landscape, with bracken instead of cacti, eerie enough in its own right but made all the more ominous by the presence of dozens of malevolent goats, some of them silhouetted on high ledges, others poking around on the slopes, and one particular creature that scrambles up the hillside onto the path and struts in front of us for several hundred yards, apparently ushering us out of its territory. They're semi-feral, content to nibble and munch their way around their own domain, except in winter, when they roam into Lynton and dine in the parks and gardens, much to the annoyance of residents. I once lived next door to a goat farm and have avoided the animals ever since, the main reason being the smell of their urine, a stringent, vinegar-

and-chloride stench that makes cat pee smell like Chanel No. 5 by comparison and which lingers on in goat cheese and goat milk, at least according to my nose. The beast leading us west this morning has the look and bearing of a regimental mascot, implying a certain level of restraint or even tameness, but is also the owner of horribly pointed horns and powerful haunches. When it glances backwards it has enough of the devil in the horizontal slots of its pupils to suggest it could inflict serious damage if it were contradicted or crossed. Where the pass narrows, as well as the stocky males there are a couple of dozen females dotted here and there and kids sleeping on stony platforms to all sides. The stink of piss-flavoured chèvre curdling in the morning sun is nauseating. The path dips into the grounds of Lee Abbey, a Christian conference and activity centre, and tennis courts to the right stand like a symbol of the death of English tennis, private and empty, defended on three sides by Satan's representative animal here on Earth and by unscaleable cliffs on the other. Behind them, in a little patch of Golgotha on the North Devon coast, between spiky clumps of gorse, three vacant wooden crosses stand silhouetted on the horizon, awaiting their sinners.

Woods follow. The hillsides have an alpine feel to them on occasions, and where stone steps rise steeply under giant ferns, across tumbling streams and past glittering waterfalls, among lilies and orchids, we could be climbing towards more exotic and faraway locations. Any moment now we might break surface on the upper reaches of Kilimanjaro or among the ruins of Machu Picchu. Through gaps in the trees and leaves we stand and gawp at the biggest views of the sea so far, one hundred and eighty degrees of turquoise water

under an electric-blue sky. Stretching away in front, the
coast lies scalloped and crenulated for a distance of maybe
twenty miles, headlands followed by cliffs followed by bays,
followed by headlands followed by cliffs followed by bays,
like splayed toes or a long thick crust bitten and chomped by
the hungry ocean. It's a mesmerising and seductive vision,
but it also marks the beginning of the peaks and troughs that
characterise so much of this national trail, those unremitting
gradients and inclines which will only increase in frequency
and severity from this point forward and are said to test the
calves and knee joints of even the fittest walkers. The first
such examination arrives in the form of Heddon's Mouth,
with the track tootling along nonchalantly until the sudden,
unannounced lacuna of the Heddon Valley. The path almost
delivers us into the abyss before swerving inland then
descending diagonally towards the landing strip of a mown
field and a small, tree-sheltered bridge. Then it's a tortuous
pull up the other side, one of those ascents which causes complete bodily ache, even in the gums and roots of the teeth.
Half an hour later we're finally back at the same height, but
have travelled no more than five hundred yards in a straight
line. Environmental concerns aside, if ever there was a case
for a suspension bridge or even a zip wire this would be it, an
architectural fantasy I'll have perhaps a hundred times more
over the coming weeks. I'm last to the top and suggest a picnic, largely as an excuse for letting my blood fall below boiling point and the timpani solo in my ears subside. Carolynn
and Roland have succumbed to the temptation of the Hunt-
er's Inn and diverted inland. John is 'beanpole' in stature.
He's using the rubberised pannier from his bike as a day
bag, which slung over his shoulder gives him the look of an

overgrown paperboy a long way from the nearest letter box. Whenever a butterfly lands on a flower he stoops over it from his great height and inspects it through the wide lenses of his dark-framed glasses, which extend horizontally beyond the narrow profile of his face. He's in a competition with a friend to spot the most British butterfly species in a year, and is stuck on twenty-one. Rob is a regular runner on these cliffs; he used to live near by and knows another side to North Devon, one not always apparent to holidaymakers and visitors. Not long ago he was taking an early-morning jog along the coast path when he was confronted by a disembodied stag's head jammed on top of a signpost, its eyes looking in different directions and an indescribable slop of bloody, steaming innards dangling and dripping from its severed neck. All part of a cat-and-mouse game between the police trying to impose hunting restrictions and arrogant local hunters asserting their right to kill. Three years ago a photograph emerged of a nine-foot-tall red stag with fourteen-point antlers, estimated to weigh around three hundred pounds. Christened 'the Emperor of Exmoor', a few days later it was reported shot by trophy hunters determined to bag 'Britain's biggest wild animal'. A mounted head believed to be that of the Emperor eventually appeared on the wall of a nearby hotel, but was removed after the owner received death threats. Away from the bloodshed and gratuitous slaughter the region also attracts its fair share of alternative thinkers and UFO-spotters. Holdstone Down is a particular draw, the place where Dr George King, founder of the Aetherius Society (strapline: 'Co-operating with the Gods from Space'), was visited by Jesus in 1958, who 'appeared before him in radiant physical form'. Of the nineteen mountains worldwide held in holy esteem by the Society, Hold-stone Hill is the most sacred, and on 23 July of each year its membership congregate around the summit and recharge their batteries with the cosmological energy and spiritual power emanating from its core. From the path, the nipple of the cairn at the very top is just visible to the naked eye. Before the descent of Sherrycombe I find and photograph a dead slow-worm, mangled or chewed at the tail end but with head and eyes perfectly preserved, placing my four-foot hol-ly stick next to its five or six inches of sun-dried, brown-grey body for the purpose of scale. After which it's another heart-bursting trek to the peak of Great Hangman, all 314 metres of it, plus a few metres more of stone rubble and scree that form an improvised cairn at the top and afford a spectacular view of the coastline in both directions. In front, Swansea and Tenby are visible on the far side of the wide and empty Bristol Channel. Behind, the backdrop is the undulating spine of Dartmoor, a much darker horizon overshadowed by murky clouds and planted with wind turbines. Another landmark, and one which will become a companion and coordinate for many days to come, is Lundy, low and elon-gated and isolated out there in the shining water.

Sue has strained a 'downhill muscle' and can only manage the descent by means of a crab-like, sideways movement, or by walking backwards down the narrow track, where brambles and elderberry have intertwined and overarched to form a dizzying tube or chute. Above Combe Martin's double-fronted beach we're discharged into the top corner of a field or public 'rec', where a couple on a blanket are fla-grantly indulging in what used to be referred to as heavy petting and was one of several banned activities at my local swimming pool, along with running, bombing and smoking. A scouting party sent to look for me are waiting by the ticket machine in the car park. They've already approached seven or eight 'possibles', but it's the hat that persuades them I might be the poet they're looking for. They walk me through a heaving crowd of day-trippers, weekend visitors and summer holidaymakers to a guest house on the other side of town decorated with Union flag bunting. There's a metal tray on the floor in the entrance to receive hot and dusty boots, next to a fire extinguisher underneath a noticeboard advertising a recital by 'The Wandering Poet'.

*

Penny and John run Mellstock House Bed and Breakfast. John also volunteers for Combe Martin Museum, where I'm reading, in the Sail Loft, surrounded by stuffed gulls, wooden oars, sea-life posters, a grocer's bicycle, a display of fishing rods and a working interactive model of a pulley system. John closes the sliding doors in front of the glass fire exit so I'm not upstaged by gurning youths or groping adolescents during the performance. Before the second half he says to me, 'Shall I introduce you again, in case people have forgotten who you are?', and during the interval a silver-haired lady presses a small coin into my palm and closes my fingers around it with her hand. Have I just accepted the Queen's shilling? Rob, now divested of his hiking gear and sitting in the audience in a Fred Perry T-shirt and trainers, looks as thin as a drink of water, and John the cyclist is even thinner. In fact the leanness and fitness of those two young men probably explains why we covered today's mileage in such a

short space of time, why Sue is limping, why I feel so knackered and why my back is aching. Note to self: fell runners
and long-distance cyclists not ideal walking companions.
Alison from Areas of Outstanding Natural Beauty (AONB),
who are supporting and promoting some of the readings,
has brought me a couple of their T-shirts, one large and one
extra large. 'It was difficult to tell from your photographs.'
After drinks and nibbles on the ground floor, served next to
the Science Pod and among the relics and artefacts that
make up the Combe Martin Story exhibition, it's back to
Mellstock House and a seat at the bar. In his Manc/Scouse/
Welsh accent John tells me the property was named after
Thomas Hardy's 'Afternoon Service at Mellstock', a framed
copy of which hangs in the hall. 'We were going to name
each room after a Hardy poem, but they're all so effing
gloomy.' He reports that business is pretty good, but it's
against the backdrop of a community struggling against
cuts, closures, poor summers and the never-ending recession. The museum has merged with the Information Centre and is staffed by volunteers. The local baker has just shut
up shop, and the place is 'dead' in winter. 'We might call
your room the Armitage Suite,' he shouts after me up the
stairs. Inside the Armitage Suite, Mrs Armitage is none too
pleased with an item left in the sock, a message from someone called Naomi who is looking forward to intercepting
me en route, though the card it's written on is the type usually pinned on a wreath or accompanying a roadside bou-
quet. 'Maybe it's you that should be worried, not me,' she
says, then turns out the light.

Combe Martin to Woolacombe

14.25 MILES

Sunday 1 September

The distances are getting longer, and so are the days. To walk over fourteen miles and arrive in time to eat, scrub up and get my head together for the next reading means an early start and no dawdling. Which could spell trouble for someone carrying a 'downhill muscle' injury, especially if the contours of the map are to be believed. After the now customary hug and photograph with landlord and landlady we walk out into the new month, the weather still holding up after several unbroken weeks of proper, old-fashioned summer, the outlook promising. The forecast on my mobile phone shows a full house of beaming sunshine symbols, something I don't remember seeing since I was in the Middle East, a brightness to illuminate the classic coastal scenery promised by the guidebook. But first a hill, then what feels like a trespass through a camping and caravan site set back from the cliffs. From either side comes the sound of zips being unzipped, the sense of taut fabric relaxing, and the sight of sleepy families stumbling through flaps into the light of morning and the dewy grass. Collapsible tables and folding chairs are being assembled around cool-boxes and portable stoves. Tea towels and swimwear are drip-drying on awnings and guy ropes. Some of the tents are little more than pop-up igloos or playhouses, but get bigger and grander where the path curves through what must be a more exclusive quarter. Here are annexes, porticoes, vestibules, colonnades and tents which are merely the porches or lobbies to monster-size motorhomes with TV aerials on the roof and surfboards or mountain bikes lashed to rear-mounted frames. As if in admonishment, a lone tepee made from torn and stitched canvas has squeezed into a gap between two of the marquees, with a Citroën 2CV parked next to it, its offside wheel arch patched with a flattened Coke can. Rose hips and palm trees line the way, with beech and hazel flanking the path towards the bottom gate. The smell in the air alternates between Calor Gas and fried bacon. After Watermouth Bay and some wilfully quirky signposting, the path disgorges us into a muddy harbour at low tide, with two dozen boats either propped on stilts or grounded or beached, leaning at precarious angles, their underbellies rudely displayed to the world. Like wading birds we have to pick our way across the watery runnels and brackish gloop, following instinct rather than instructions towards a rusting arrow on the far side of the bay. Then up, then down, then up, then down. On the descents, Sue's compromised walking style has now developed into something resembling one of the more recherché elements of horse dressage, a peculiar diagonal movement beginning with an exaggerated stride followed by a half twist, then a flick of the hips which brings the trailing leg level with the leading foot. A party of hikers going in the opposite direction give her a funny look then give me a funny look as well; with my big stick I probably appear to be some heartless drover, bullying his stricken creature towards market. And despite all reassurances to the contrary the gradients only become steeper and more frequent. After Hele Bay, the winding path to the top of Hillsborough is an unforgiving, endless upward spiral through a precipitous wood choked with ivy and shadow. It's the kind of ascent that might come with all sorts of warnings and exclamation marks were it the concluding mile of some epic pilgrimage or even the single climb towards a famous beauty spot, but on this path it barely warrants a mention. A wooden bench about two-thirds of the way to the summit offers an elevated view of the sea when an oxygen tank and a masseuse would have been more welcome.

*

Ilfracombe gets a bad press in these parts. The name appears to be a byword among locals for the downbeat or the downright rough, and its three syllables are often enunciated within invisible speech marks. All population centres of whatever size need a place to belittle and disparage, either through historical grievances, local rivalries, ill-informed prejudices or out of some more primitive human tendency to define our own status in terms of a neighbour's shortcomings. In this region Ilfracombe has landed that role, or at least had it thrust upon it. That it's a particularly faded and failed Victorian seaside resort seems to be the polite version, though this might be a smokescreen masking an uglier attitude towards the number of benefit claimants said to be renting the town's otherwise unoccupied holiday accommodation – not what more genteel folks thought they were buying into when they retired to the North Devon coast. I've tested the word 'Ilfracombe' on several people so far, even tried it out at the reading last night, and on every occa-

sion it caused eyes to roll or eyebrows to rise, though one of
its residents did respond with the spirited comment, 'Well,
it's better than being a Combe Martian.' From the top of
Hillsborough, Ilfracombe looks alive and well down in the
bay, and increasingly vibrant as we walk towards it, though
it's true that most towns look happy and healthy in the sunshine, of which there is no shortage this morning, and no
shortage of tourists either, today being the last day of the
school holidays. Most people appear to be heading for the
statue on the pier, visible from several miles away and at
that distance an assertive, classical, upright form with a
raised sword, a dramatic and unexpected symbol of power
and pride that wouldn't look out of place at the entrance to
the Corinth Canal or on a mountain above a latter-day
metropolis. When craned into position last year, Damien
Hirst's steel and bronze *Verity* was the tallest free-standing
sculpture in Britain, a mischievous one foot higher than
Antony Gormley's *Angel of the North* and in some ways a
visual rejoinder to that piece. In size and scale it looks whol-
ly incongruous above the little harbour and beyond the
avenue of ice-cream parlours and tea shops. But bold, and
astonishingly graphic on closer inspection, because those
visitors inquisitive enough to venture around the front elevation are gradually confronted with the image of a nude,
heavily pregnant woman whose right side appears to have
been peeled of skin, revealing the anatomy and musculature
beneath. Her unborn foetus lies in the exposed cross-section
of the womb and to look upwards is to look at a head which
is half face and half skull, indifferent and anonymous in one
profile, grotesque and gruesome in the other. In a thick
Midlands accent the woman standing next to me says to her

husband, 'She looks like your mother,' and the man nods. The public reaction to the semi-flayed figure has been as divided as *Verity* herself, with the appalled and the inspired arguing back and forth through the letters pages of the *North Devon Gazette* and across social media. Personally, I like the piece. It might lack subtlety or seem a touch petulant in its attempt to shock, and at certain angles does look like the cover image from a teen-oriented graphic novel in which zombie robots stalk the planet. But desperate measures call for daring actions; tourist numbers are up, and a pound is a pound, whether from the pocket of a discerning art critic, a rubbernecking voyeur or a Birmingham daughter-in-law noticing family resemblances. Ilfracombe doesn't own the sculpture, it's on loan for twenty years, but my hunch is that by 2023 *Verity*, or at least the presentable side of her, will have become the town's adopted daughter and even the logo on the council's letterhead.

It's a hot day and it's getting hotter. In her own way Sue is also half a woman right now, limping along courageously, dragging her useless leg behind her and leaving some decidedly enigmatic tracks across sandier stretches of the path, like a row of semicolons. Heading uphill she's fine, and on the way out of Ilfracombe we don't even stop to look back to compare the bizarre double cones of the Landmark Theatre with the cooling towers that once stood alongside the M1 between Sheffield and Rotherham – presumably not the architectural reference point when the theatre was first conceived. But on the descents she's having problems, so much so that dropping into Lee Bay we have to stand aside to let an old man with a Zimmer frame go past. The Lee Bay Hotel, which dominates the small valley and to the approaching visitor *is* Lee Bay, also appears to be heading downhill and struggling as a consequence. Abandoned and derelict behind a mesh security fence it might even have hit rock bottom. With its boarded-up doors, fallen-in roof and weed-infested patios, a set designer couldn't have put together a more cli-chéd monument to the themes of ruination and demise, and a poster on one of the broken windows reads, 'NO CASH ON SITE'. Even the sign on the gate looks like it came from the props department of a cheesy, low-budget film company, a rust-streaked and woodworm-eaten board with the hotel name hand-painted in excreta brown, minus its first and last letters. Down in the pebbly bay a man is trying to convince his young son they are on holiday by getting him to throw small stones at bigger stones. I'm beginning to recognise how no two valleys are alike on this walk, even when they lie next door to each other. So a few miles further along we enter a more tranquil, slightly unworldly location, an unsung and as far as I can tell unnamed inlet to the back of Damagehue Rock. There's no road to here, just a grassy sward track curving along the nick of the marshy valley, half hidden by bracken, and a sunken stream running alongside, overgrown with rushes, reeds and meadow flowers. A wooden pontoon bridge spans the water where the stream pools and slows, and the bay to the seaward side is dotted with moss-coated stones and bigger rocks like seats or thrones facing Wales, the view funnelled and framed by cliffs to each side. A pen-sive, enclosed, contemplative place, empty of human traffic and spared any touristy intervention. Not off the map exact-ly but out of the way and out of the wind, so traversing it feels like a form of immersion, a few minutes of particular self-consciousness and sensory awareness, a recognition of the future memory of this location already developing like a photograph, a scene that will stay in the mind, which we pass through in shared silence. Its relevance is also heightened in a cartographical sense because it marks the moment when the boom of the horizon swings across and the path tacks decisively to the port side, heading south-west after days of walking virtually due west, soon to swing even further to the south. It's progress of a kind, a new direction for the time being, a new map and a change of view. Even though Lundy remains a stretched, low-lying form in the distance, pink cliffs to this side give it the appearance of a new, yet-to-be-explored land mass, and the body of water beyond the shore has expanded beyond the confines of the Bristol Channel into what might plausibly be thought of as the Atlantic Ocean.

The lighthouse on the promontory of Bull Point must have been positioned here with those same sight lines in mind. Clean and monastic in its white-walled compound and with its white-walled buildings it could be its own contained community, comprising a modern bungalow, two or three garages, outbuildings, a meticulously manicured lawn, a short tarmacked lane and a row of single-storey coastguard cottages which are now holiday lets. From our picnic position on a mound level with the top of the lighthouse we catch disarming glimpses of the fins and facets of the huge lens as it rolls and revolves in its housing, like the eye of a giant insect whose attentions we would do well to avoid.

It's still hot. The hottest part of the day in fact, without shelter or shade. Sue hobbles forward, and I'm not exactly skipping along myself. Morte Point is the next objective, a jagged headland of bright, exposed rocks spearing into the sea, vivid and adamantine in the late afternoon sun. It's a bumpy, twisty, hilly path to get there, a path that dissipates among the tooth-coloured stones, worn and polished by the soles of a million walkers, the route having no option but to drop down onto the lower contours and follow the high-water mark around the formation, which is a point both in nature and name. Around the corner Woolacombe is still over a mile away, which translates as an hour or so at this pace. We're a couple who try to live in the present whenever and wherever we can, but every once in a while we have discussed the future, a future with more walking in it and less work, and perhaps this is a rehearsal of its later stages, the two of us shuffling lamely into the sunset. Though if old age or the afterlife turn out to be the equivalent of the Woolacombe Bay Hotel, then I wouldn't mind so much. It's probably the only time on the whole journey that I'll have access to complimentary pencils and biscuits, and definitely the only time I'll be assisted by a bellhop. As well as drag-ging the Galapagos Tortoise into the room, dropped off by John from Mellstock House, he also delivers bad news regarding the outcome of a sporting contest taking place in the opposite part of the country, a contest I'd told myself I wasn't interested in, here on the South West Coast Path with my mind on higher things, but which depresses me once I've heard the result. I steep in the bath for an hour while Sue goes in search of 'therapy' – a sauna plus essential oils, I assume, rather than a session with a Jungian analyst, but either way, when she comes back to the room she declares herself to be 'mended'. Perfectly composed in the window and in the arms of the bay, Lundy looks like a plinth from which a statue has been stolen. I call Sue over to

look at two seals in the sea, which are seals only until they stand up and walk onto the beach in their black rubber wet-suits. Frogmen, as they used to be called, especially on news bulletins when they were looking for bodies in reservoirs and canals.

Paul is very tall. I accidentally call him 'Tall' at one point: 'Shall I put this bag in the boot, Tall?' but he doesn't hear or he's kind enough not to reply. We drive inland to Georgeham, to the village hall, and en route my tongue slips a couple more times, not quite in synch with my thoughts. Mild exhaustion, possibly? Too many free bis-cuits? Maybe the bath was too hot? Outside the hall there's a sundial on the wall with a faded poem carved into the faded wood, something about 'when we are gone' and 'love lives on'. I'm definitely in the right place because there's a poster on the noticeboard promoting tonight's event, next to an advert for 'Heartstart' classes ('Would you know what to do in a life-threatening emergency?') and the local mobile library schedule. Inside, though, it's all a bit fuzzy, a bit ill-defined. I'm on stage under a light, and feel as if I'm falling continually forward. I make a 'joke' and nobody laughs. Rather than going off-message I decide to stick to the script and just read the poems, and they seem to be making sense, and yet there's a kind of delay between what I say and what I hear myself say, like a transatlantic satellite phone call, except the distance here isn't several thousand miles but a matter of inches between my mouth and my ears. Even the photograph I take of the audience (my way of recording attendance figures) is blurred, like one image superimposed on the other but not quite aligned, or as if everyone in the hall had suddenly vibrated at the same time. I'm not sure if the eighty-odd people in front of me are aware of my own malfunctioning, but I'm definitely not myself, not even after the reading, when I find myself strongly disagreeing with a man about Leonard Cohen's claims to be a poet.

'Well, he's published a book of poems,' says the man.

'So has Leonard Nimoy,' I say, under my breath.

'I beg your pardon?'

Paul offers to take me for a drink but I feel very weak, and very small alongside him, and getting smaller by the minute. Back at the hotel my head is spinning, and when I clamp it in my hands to stop it wheeling and whirling the room spins instead. In my sleep, the horrible insect stares from the lamp of Bull Point lighthouse, and the Lee Bay Hotel wobbles and crashes, and *Verity* beads me with her hollow eye, and when the baby in her belly rolls over and turns its head towards me it has the face of Dr Spock. Sometime after midnight, when I've finished puking for the final time, I say, 'I think it was sunstroke.'

Sue: 'I thought you had some kind of fancy hat.'

Me: 'I have.'

Sue: 'I thought it had some sort of fancy UV protection.'

Me: 'It does.'

Sue: 'It was really expensive, wasn't it?'

Me: 'It was.'

Pause.

Sue: 'You haven't been wearing it, have you?'

Me: 'No.'

Sue: 'Why not?'

Me: 'It was too hot.'

Woolacombe to Braunton

Monday 2 September

The distances are getting longer, and so are the days. I am the only person having breakfast in the expensively decorated and expansively carpeted dining room of the Woolacombe Bay Hotel. The waitress is polite but seems suspicious, nervous even, possibly because (a) It's 7.30 in the morning, or (b) I'm wearing a hat, or (c) I've waved away an extensive menu in favour of a round of dry white toast and a cup of black tea, or (d) I'm in my stockinged feet.

'Muddy boots,' I tell her, as if that explained everything.

'OK,' she says, and heads off into the kitchen with the order. Throughout my prisoner's banquet I see the faces of other kitchen staff peering through the doorway then ducking out of sight. Sue has departed, but I'm determined to enjoy a few hours of introspection and self-indulgence, today being the first time I've been alone since Butlins, which now feels like several weeks ago. I'm also looking forward to entering those long and empty areas of the map largely devoid of form or feature, otherwise known as beaches. So far I've walked fifty miles and still haven't left a footprint in the sand or put my toe in the water, something I'm going to correct today because as far as the Ordnance Survey is concerned the landscape between here and Braunton is mostly yellow. Or something between vanilla and magnolia.

Woolacombe at eight in the morning is very quiet. A man is mopping out the public toilets and another is emptying an overflowing litter basket. Four surfers in their skin-tight outfits prance towards the shore like ballet dancers in black leotards. On the pitch 'n' putt two seagulls are having a tug of war over a crisp packet. Otherwise, it's just me. Just me hopping over the wall behind the hotel lido. Just me noticing that the fish-and-chip shack has a row of optics on the back shelf. Just me in my big boots and fancy hat with its impressive UV protection levels clomping along the front, then up a hill bordered by blackberry bushes pecked and picked clean of any fruit. And just me following the official path into the warren of dunes and humps that runs parallel to the coast and below Potter's Hill. The ground is gritty rather than sandy, and so strewn with snail shells that it's impossible to avoid stepping on them. Most crunch and dis-integrate underfoot, others emit a more upsetting squelch-ing sound. There's an oppressive and impenetrable bank of brambles forming a horizon to the left and the dunes to the right are so exaggerated and sheer that after a while I'm walking in a narrow, shadowy channel, then what feels like a trench. It's dark, claustrophobic, but more than anything it's boring, and at the first breach in the barricade I veer off and find a route through the swaying marram grass onto the beach. Which turns out to be the best decision of the day and the best move of the walk so far. It reminds me that I came here with the intention of experiencing the margin, of striding along the edge, and suddenly here it is in all its wide-open glory, the reach and fetch of it, vast and magnifi-cent. The tide might be out and the sea might be half a mile away or even more, but I feel to be below it, walking beneath a wall of water that appears to be tilted this way and might topple over at the next push of the tide. Beneath a *body* of water, and the din of the waves at its leading edge as they thrash and heave and collapse carries all the way across the flat, saturated, sun-glazed sand. It's dizzying, dazzling, and it's all for me, because in several square miles of beach the five or six other figures who inhabit this space on this wind-scrubbed glittering morning are so far away, so negligible and so insubstantial that they barely exist. And the map lied, because within those large blocks of standard OS shading the eye eventually discerns an unlimited spectrum of colour within the sand: cream, corn, gold, mustard, salmon, straw, umber, amber, peach, pearl, brass, skin, bronze, bisque, buff, tan. And discerns striations of tone and texture lying at intervals from the shoreline, like tree rings, with some strips of sand already dried by the wind and the morning sun and others still damp and heavy from last night's tide. And discerns gradations of sand, from fine powder to coarse scratchy granules. And relief patterns in the surface caused by drain-ing water or eddying breezes, domes and depressions, fur-rows and bevels, ribs and ripples, levelled plains that could have been finished with a plasterer's trowel followed by a few hundred yards of chaotic ground that looks like the aftermath of a stampede.

The firmest and easiest place to walk is across the strand, which forms a raised path about fifty yards shy of the dunes, and along here there's an even greater range of colour and shape, but one that's far less attractive. A strandline could be said to symbolise many things: the fluctuating, transitory delineation between land and sea; the story of last night's clash between turf and tide; the upper limit of the moon's

advances against the Earth's reluctance. In a depressingly
literal way the strandline along Woolacombe Sands repre-
sents the coming together of Man and Nature, because as
well as bladderwrack, feather, cuttlefish and bone, most of
what has washed up here is of human making. Striding
along it's impossible not to see it as an inventory of environmental complacency and a catalogue of shame. Plastic netting, cassette tape, oil drums, dollops of tar, a golf tee, dozens
of plastic lollipop sticks, hundreds of plastic bottles, milk
cartons, a burst balloon, tons of insoluble and indivisible
and un-biodegradable waste dumped in the dustbin of the
sea and duly returned. The list gets longer with every step,
a conveyor belt of garbage that I find myself itemising and
auditing. Medicine bottles, plastic cups, plastic glasses, plastic straws, knotted plastic bags with God knows what inside
them, T-shirts, underpants, socks, sandals, fishing line,
floats, buoys, toothbrushes, leather, rubber, Styrofoam,

polystyrene, nylon, deflated inner tubes, deflated footballs, deflated beach balls, deflated inflatables, inflated condoms, a crust of detritus stretching from one end of the bay to the other. Even from the high fields going out along the next hill I can still see its trail, its multicoloured disfiguring scar. And can still make out the many colours of the beach, which triggers a memory or flashback to the ladies' section of Kaye's department store in Huddersfield in the late sixties, where I'm standing with my mother next to the revolving display of tights and stockings. Each packet has a little cellophane window showing the shade of nylon, which she holds in her glove as she matches it against the complexion of her bare leg.

*

The cliffs above the beach are a fine place to be, but there's a sameness to this kind of walking, with the corner of my right eye always full of the blueness of the water and my left always full of the greenness of the land, and the path a narrow and occasionally precarious tightrope down the middle that has to be watched and negotiated. Also, the natural camber of the coast means that my right leg is always further down the hill than my left and is theoretically doing more work and walking further, especially around a headland like Baggy Point, which demands a hundred-and-eighty-degree about-turn. I might even end up with one leg longer than the other, like people who live on the side of mountains, or like the Scottish haggis. Below the cliffs a couple of joggers who arrived from different directions are kissing and cuddling behind a large rock. They think I can't see them but I can, even though I'm not watching. My dad phones to say good morning. It's ten thirty and I can tell from his voice that he's lying in bed.

Dave Edgecombe from North Devon Coast AONB is waiting for me in a car park before Croyde Beach. He's wearing jogging bottoms and a pair of beaten-up trainers, so I guess we aren't going anywhere too expeditionary. Croyde has a particular reputation in these parts, immediately reinforced by the presence of half a dozen well-moisturised teenage boys with public-school haircuts, loafing on their surfboards and enjoying the sound of their own nicknames by the roadside cafe. Dave's accent, to my ear, is soft Devon. On Croyde Sands, in the throat of the bay between Baggy Point and Saunton Down, he tells me that these beaches were used by the US army for landing training prior to D-Day, the topography being similar to the coast of Normandy, and points to a couple of dummy pillboxes which were practice targets for taking out German gun positions. There was a big reunion last weekend, and if I'd been here yesterday I would have seen a Sherman tank. There's no sign of any military hardware this morning, not even a pair of caterpillar tracks, just a volleyball net and seven or eight more surfers, clones of the previous batch, trying to play volleyball without spilling their takeaway cappuccinos. I splash through a wide delta of fresh water, and Dave has to track upstream to find a fording point. He catches me up on terra firma, where the path squeezes along a narrow strip between low cliffs on one side and a barbed-wire fence on the other. Coastal erosion is a major headache for all guardians of the trail, and even though the tide is out and the sea looks incapable of even mild petulance on a day like today, the rate at which the land is crumbling is increasing decade on decade, with weathering more severe and storms more frequent. Every landslip and rockfall means going cap in hand (or cheque book in pocket) to the land owner, to try to negotiate a few extra yards. Failing that, a new route has to be plotted, often involving a detour away from the coast, sometimes along a busy road. Several sections of the trail are currently closed after the deluges of last summer, even more on the south coast along stretches where the path is deemed to be unsafe or has disappeared altogether. In that respect, the coast path is only an idea, a conceptual possibility rather than a fixed line in the Earth's surface, a right of way only where a way exists, or where permission allows, or where Dave and his kind have been able to prop up the cliffs, chop back the gorse or cadge a bit of field. His other headache is the proposed Atlantic Array, an offshore wind farm that would dominate the vista from this part of the coast. If construction goes ahead, two hundred and forty turbines will occupy a site of about eighty square miles between here and South Wales, bisecting the horizon. Eight miles from Lundy, at 220 metres high they would stand taller than the island itself, whose eastern cliffs look like ski slopes in this morning's sun. The power cables will have to be brought ashore somewhere around here, and Dave wonders out loud if there's any point in designating somewhere a Site of Special Scientific Interest or an Area of Outstanding Natural Beauty or a Special Area of Conservation or a National Park if the bulldozers can simply roll up one morning and begin tearing into the ground. He's well versed in the arguments about renewable energy and it's beyond his pay grade to start lobbying against engineering projects that aren't strictly on his patch, but the idea of an oceanic city of alien superstructures taking centre stage in the amphitheatre of this coastline and in the middle of a view that hasn't changed for a million years certainly troubles his soul. He puts his hand over his eyes and we move on, taking the alternative 'ruined barn' route up and along the flank of Saunton Down, partly to avoid plodding through Saunton itself and partly for the view across the beaches, dunes, marshes, mud-flats, links, inlets, dykes and the matrix of Braunton Great Field, a vivid patchwork of oblong enclosures that lies to the south. Dave also points out the greater peninsula stretching away to the south-west, an elongated, steep-sided plateau with thickly wooded slopes, punctuated by the huddled buildings of Bucks Mills and Clovelly and two or three less-er communities all the way to the spur of Hartland Point, which looks like the end of the world. Miles of coast path, days of walking, a sort of diary or itinerary in physical, geo-graphical form, laid out in front. 'It looks like a long way,' I tell Dave. 'Right. And you're not even there yet,' he says, somewhat gnomically. He gestures towards a sandy track on the other side and says, 'It's down there,' and off I go.

By 'it' he means *the way*, I guess. But he could also mean Braunton Burrows, which is very much an 'it', a thing in its own right, with a presence and atmosphere unlike any oth-er territory on this walk, but difficult to categorise and not quickly traversed. In fact I am in 'it' for the next four pon-derous and at times hallucinatory hours, at one point stum-bling onto a golf green, at one point passing two nuns picking blackberries, at one point stepping over a dead fox, at one point entering a military training area with a warn-ing sign depicting three armed commandos, at one point being tailed by a bull terrier with the body of a small pony and the head of a tyrannosaurus rex, and at one point walking alongside a barbed-wire fence decorated with a selection of impaled fruit. It might be low blood sugar following last night's vomiting marathon. Or it might be the sun, which is on full beam, right in my face, though I am wearing my fancy hat. But I honestly think it's the landscape, the dunes swelling and rising on one side, queasy marshes and swamps on the other, long arrowing sections of stony track with loose hard core underfoot, a jag to the right into a boggy copse, then a jag to the left into an open heath, and always a sense of being below sea level, under unusual barometric conditions, breathing stale air. Braunton Burrows is a *zone*, a *sector*, a puzzle of high hedges, unwavering paths leading towards vanishing points somewhere in the middle distance, and long flat meadows with no landmark to break them and no resolution before the blurred infinity of the

heat-hazed horizon. I wouldn't want to be here in the mist or the dark; it feels like somewhere the police might comb with sniffer dogs and the help of volunteers, without reward. The same clump of evening primrose goes past about four or five times. The golf course reappears again; a squat, almost square man in brown brogues, white knee socks and banana-yellow Bermuda shorts stands on the raised platform of the tee, his beer belly expanding the diamond pattern on his woollen tank top to its elastic limit. Before he drives, his playing partner, in similarly psychedelic colours, rings a bell – a polished brass dome mounted on a post with a length of rope dangling from the clapper, like a ship's bell – and its mournful sounds drift out across the sandy fairways. Then they set off under the canopy of their two-man motorised buggy, like a pair of out-of-work clowns looking for a circus. It's well into the afternoon when I stumble onto the spit of Crow Point, where the land peters out in a series of exposed sand bars and glittering, burping mud. About half a dozen boats are either moored or marooned, some just dozing, waiting for the return of the tide, others rusting and rotting away, waiting for the maritime equivalent of a vulture to pick them clean. Picnicking here with the map out in front of me, studying the ill-defined features of Shellhook, Pulley Ridge, South Gut, Yell Pool and The Neck, I begin to understand what Dave said a few hours ago, about not being there yet. Because even though Appledore looks to be within touching distance on the other side, the South West Coast Path now turns north-east along the Taw estuary. I have to unfold the map then unfold it twice more before arriving at the first bridging point, way off in Barnstaple, by which time the mouth of the Torridge has also opened up, meaning a further inland excursion, this time to Bideford, and in total some two and a half days' walking for progress of about a mile and a half, as the crow flies. The confluence of the Taw and the Torridge must produce deep water and strong currents, but after a hot summer and with the tide as far out as it is today there's only a slow running stream in the narrow channel between the mudflats. Hardly a trickle. And although the orthodox route rounds the cape and heads for safety, an alternative route, indicated on the map with distinctive green dashes, wiggles and winds enticingly onto the sand and ends with a green diamond, like a snake's head, at the Mean High Water mark, next to the word 'groynes'. What if, what if? A big black dog comes bounding up to a woman reading a book in the dunes, knocking her face-first into the ground. 'Kaiser, Kaiser, leave her alone,' its owner is calling from a couple of hundred yards away, and the woman is saying, 'Don't worry, it's fine,' with a mouthful of sand and a hundredweight of wolfhound straddling her shoulders.

The path to Braunton is along the top of a raised breakwater. Curlew and redshank are feeding in the acres of silt, and on the other side half a dozen sheep have strayed onto the banks to nibble at weeds sprouting through the crust of mud. Jetties and piers step off into the river bed then end abruptly in mid-air, like bridges that have run out of courage. The flooded meadows on the left are reminiscent of a broads or fenland topography. Where the toecap and the outer wall of my left boot were once stitched together a big hole now opens and closes its fish lips with every step, and a smaller hole in the same position on my right boot winks in reply. Cattle are standing about indolently under a bridge,

as they would in a Constable painting. Houseboats tied to mooring posts or trees lean at gravity-defying angles – it must be dangerous to boil a kettle on board, and impossible to leave a melon or egg on a worktop. A sloshing, gurgling sound in the shallow water signals the return of the sea, the first nudge of the incoming tide against the outflowing stream, just a slow churning at first, a rumour of some great turnaround out in the Atlantic that in an hour's time will have grown to a full-scale invasion, the retreating river being chased by saltwater threatening to surge as far as its source. There's no poetry section in Braunton Library, or if there is it's well hidden, so no Armitage. According to a poster in the window advertising local talks I'm up against 'Devon's Hedgerows and Their Wildlife' and 'The Fantastic World of Fungi' tonight, though my reading is a few miles from here in oxymoronically named Swimbridge. A Volvo estate pulls into the car park, and the man at the wheel with the looking-for-a-poet expression on his face must be Geoffrey.

*

Geoffrey doesn't strike me as a Geoffrey, more of a Bradley with his cyclist's physique and Wiggo sideburns. He lives in a converted Baptist chapel. In fact *he* converted it, from a sacred building to a family house, though one given over to the worship of bicycles, which lean against the wooden panelling or hang from hooks on the walls or dangle from the high ceiling. Geoffrey is one of those people who look taller when they're sitting down. Out of the car and standing in the enormous, open-plan, split-level living room he's no bigger than me, though certainly leaner, lean like one of his pared-down, high-performance, aerodynamic racing machines, yet he lifts the Galapagos Tortoise with ease and runs with it up the wood and steel staircase, disappearing into the roof. The whole family are nut-brown from a two-wheeled holiday across France – they even rode from home to the ferry termi- nal. Kirsty and the three kids, who all have their mother's yellow hair, are in the kitchen making blackberry and apple crumble, the kids vying for first lick of the mixing spoon. The blackberries were picked in a nearby field, the apples from a branch from next door's tree, which cranes over the back garden. The front garden is a graveyard. A couple of widows still have permission to join their husbands in the soil, but apart from the occasional person paying respects or researching family history it's just an ordinary plot of land in Geoffrey's eyes. He strims it twice a year and he's happy to tidy up a grave if someone asks him to, and equally happy to install a rabbit hutch in one corner and grow runner beans between the stone slabs. An old chap originally from Moss- ley in Greater Manchester has arrived two hours too early for the reading but is offered biscuits and a book to read rather than being turned away, while we eat in the kitchen, light from the tall, torpedo-shaped chapel window falling across the room, the kids warming to the idea of a man who writes poems sitting at the head of the table and helping himself to the cheese and tomato flan. Not that guests and strangers are unusual at Heavenly House; every once in a while they open as a pop-up restaurant, with Kirsty cooking up a feast and Geoffrey playing front of house with a waiter's apron tied around his middle and sommelier's towel over his arm. On an original wooden noticeboard, under the carved heading of HYMNS, last month's menu is still on display, handwritten cards announcing Citrus Cured Salmon, Dill and Poppy Seed Soda Bread and Lemon Verbena Ice Cream where 'Shall We Gather at the River' or 'He Who Would Valiant Be' might once have appeared. I read from a black leather armchair on the upper half of the ground floor. An audience of thirty-two have turned up, including half a dozen young kids who lounge at my feet on a raft of beanbags and scatter cushions, more patient than I would have been aged seven but still a writhing and wriggling tangle of limbs, until they become many heads joined to a single restless body. Eventually one of them surreptitiously turns on an iPad and begins tapping away on the screen, her face illuminated by the glowing glass tablet. On dining chairs and settees the adults form a reverent and hushed congregation in the background.

The spare bedroom is upstairs, which in this building is *very* upstairs, though the gradient of the valley side means an unlocked door leads straight onto a lawn at the back. I wake up at five and go outside in bare feet with a pen and notebook, remembering a peculiar encounter along the side of Braunton Marsh today, thinking about stealing the forbidden fruit from the tempting bough of next door's apple tree, and being careful where I tread.

Adder

Harlequin watch-strap, Pringle sock,
selling itself
on Braunton Burrows, where dry land baulks.

Spineless spine, on its shoulderless
shoulders
all of England's slurs and lies.

The channel here runs deep
and fast, but
wing it, it lisps, *just cut across,*

you could easily save yourself
miles of slog.
Between the electrodes of its tongue

a bridgeable gap, and barely a cockstride
shore to shore
from the edge of the world to Appledore.

Braunton to Instow

Tuesday 3 September

Some walkers on the South West Coast Path find the prospect of the next two sections so unappealing and uninspiring they get on a bus and don't get off until Westward Ho!. Tied to an itinerary, compelled by completist tendencies and encouraged by the lack of contours over the forthcoming twenty or so miles there will be no recourse to public transport or any other form of vehicular conveyance on my part. Added to which, I've checked the ferry times and they don't fit my schedule, so the luminous orange line I drew across the mouth of the Torridge with a highlighter pen will remain a hypothetical flyover or subway; I'll just get my head down and walk. Geoffrey says he'll come with me for a mile or so but stays until lunchtime. By his own admission he likes to talk. 'You've probably noticed,' he says. And not just to me but to pretty much everyone between here and the other side of the river, most of whom he seems acquainted with, either because he's built a conservatory or fitted a spiral staircase or dormer window for them, or because he's known them since school, Geoffrey being one of the very few people I've met on this trip who is actually *from* here and not just a 'blow-in', as they say. Clients tend to remember him not just for the craftsmanship but because he listens to Radio 4 on site and insists his workmen keep their shirts on, 'Which comes as a disappointment to some people.'

Every ten minutes he stops to chat with somebody on the embankment, and I wander ahead while he hails a man at the side of the path and opens negotiations for the potential purchase of a Bedlington–whippet cross. At Chivenor Barracks two armed guards patrol the gate with semi-automatic weapons cradled in their arms, and a couple of brickies in vests and shorts are reinforcing the roadblock at the main entrance, one pushing a wheelbarrow with a wonky wheel and another carrying a bag of cement across his back. Geoffrey has only just caught up when he stops for another conversation, this time with a man walking his dog from the comfort of his mobility scooter, a pimped-up, top-end cabriolet model with wing mirrors, fairings, a leatherette seat and a shiny chrome frame. He's riding with the top down, making the most of the weather, and can list all the staging posts and watering holes between here and Land's End, though he won't be visiting them again, he says, not if his current symptoms persist and if the doctor keeps prescribing the same medication, which is causing his digestive system no end of problems 'at both ends'. Further along the metalled track we chat with an elderly birder with bins and a camera round his neck and a tripod over his shoulder. So far this morning he's clocked bar-tailed godwit, Mediterranean gull and greenshank, but the estuary isn't what it used to be. 'Dogging, that's the problem,' he says. 'There's a lot of it along this towpath, much more than twenty or thirty years ago, and the birds can't nest or settle, not with all that going on.' 'Dogging?' I say, not surprised that this quiet backwater should be a venue for random al fresco coupling and sexual voyeurism but alarmed to think that it should have escalated in volume or frequency to the point where it

now disrupts the breeding habits of British waders. But he just means dog-walking, and letting dogs off the leash to go careering and rampaging through the shallows and the reeds, scaring birds and scattering chicks and smashing eggs. As if to prove the point, about a mile further upstream a man is actually walking his dog *in* the river, up to his thighs in muddy water, throwing a tennis ball for his lurcher with what looks like a long-handled ice-cream scoop. From a distance he seems to be wearing a salmon-coloured top, but he's actually bare-chested, like some Old Testament character wading beyond the boundary of his parable, who set out into the cleansing currents of the Jordan and emerged in the brown sludge of the Taw where it oozes through latter-day Barnstaple. We walk into and out of the armpit of the town (I use the term geometrically, that's all) via the old, arched 'Long Bridge', which is not the ancient monument I was expecting but a fume-bound, wagon-laden road with a narrow pavement, then through Sticklepath Interchange,

North Devon's very own Spaghetti Junction, the coming together of walkways, traffic lights, slip roads and subways, all beneath a bypass growling with articulated lorries and under a roundabout groaning with the strain of a municipal art installation. Geoffrey turns back after lunch. It's probably the last time I'll be on my own for a week or so and I'm looking forward to the solitariness and silence, though it's hard to go more than a few hundred yards along the Tarka Trail without the 'ting ting' of a bicycle coming up behind, sometimes a lone senior citizen out for a pedal, sometimes a crocodile of kids wobbling along behind a teacher, sometimes Miss Marple with a wicker basket on the handlebars, and sometimes a peloton of hard-core racers who flash past in Lycra leotards, bug-eyed sunglasses and entomologically inspired helmets, like a swarm of insects. I've heard a rumour that a Hungarian translator is hoping to intercept me at the next tea shop, but nobody at Fremington Quay Café and Heritage Centre looks like they want to discuss the difficulties of exporting obscure Yorkshire idioms into a Uralic tongue, and to make sure they don't I've zipped my fleece past my chin and pulled my hat over my face. I deviate through Home Farm Marsh, detour around Isley Marsh nature reserve, dilly-dally trying to take the perfect photograph of a small blue butterfly flitting from bush to bush, dawdle in a floodplain of dried teasels standing tall and withered like the incinerated citizens of a fried planet, construct a few Goldsworthy-style vertical cairns with discus-shaped stones along the shore, and wave my holly stick at a white bull in a meadow of daisies, which looks like a big blob of lard from the path but might metamorphose into a mass of rippling muscles and thundering hoofs if I can goad it into life. In fact I procrastinate for as long as possible, despite which I'm in Instow by the indecently and inconveniently early hour of 2 p.m. I buy the widest newspaper the local deli has to offer and sit on the terrace of the colonial-style Commodore Hotel, daydreaming, looking beyond the flagpole and palm trees towards giraffes loping across the savannah, zebras on the lower slopes, alligators basking in the shallows and a sunburnt Geordie trying to wrangle a pop-up tent back into its bag. By five o'clock the sky is still a brilliant blue. Sunlight skitters and dances on the incoming tide, and moored boats in the bay are stirring and righting themselves like horses after sleep. From the passenger window of a car heading south, Dartmoor is a long barrow on the horizon.

*

David at Yarde Orchard Bunkhouse was one of the first
people to offer me a bed for the night. Unfortunately he had
to sell up at short notice due to family ill-health, and not
only are the new owners in the middle of unpacking a lifetime's possessions and getting their new business up and
running, they now have the added burden of a sponging
poet requesting a cup of tea and asking to borrow a towel.
The Bunkhouse is a series of timber buildings, yurts and
tepees catering for walkers and cyclists coming and going
along the Tarka Trail, a figure-of-eight track along North
Devon's disused railway lines that is said to follow the route
taken by Tarka the otter in Henry Williamson's book of the
same name. Two blond-haired boys are running around
their new playground, which is also their new home, and a
pair of extremely impressive wolfhounds, Hern and Orla,
are cruising the grounds like great white sharks with legs.
The woman in the cafe looks stressed but believes enough of
my unlikely story to make me a meal, which I eat outside,
under Tibetan prayer flags and home-made bunting running the length of the site, strung between every available
pole and fruit tree, hanging limp and lifeless in the sticky,
airless afternoon. My digs are in one of the lower cabins,
beyond the communal clay oven but before the campsite.
There's a double bed in the room but also a bunk bed, as if I
shouldn't count on being alone. I'm collected and driven to
Great Torrington for the only 'formal' reading of the whole
expedition, formal in the sense that it's part of a programmed
and ticketed (i.e. no sock) season of events at the Plough
Arts Centre which includes film, music, comedy and other
shows doing the rounds or currently on tour. There don't
seem to be many people in the building, even though the

event is due to start in ten minutes, and when I ask the organiser how tickets sales have been going, he thinks for a moment, as if leafing through a mental thesaurus for a word which is both socially acceptable and mathematically accurate, before replying, 'Slow.' On those relatively few occasions when he has come with me, my dad, with his thespian background and showbiz mindset, has always been distinctly underwhelmed by the lack of razzmatazz surrounding the modern poetry reading. And I can imagine him tutting or shaking his head tonight as I shuffle into the spotlight, like a roadie sent onto the stage to fix the microphone, which is exactly what I have to do for the first five minutes while trying to balance a pile of books under my arm and make unamplified small talk with the audience.

*

About a year ago I picked my daughter up from school in the car, and after we'd driven for a few minutes along the country lane that skirts Castle Hill before plunging towards Huddersfield she said, 'Aren't we going the wrong way?'
    The father: 'We're going to a garage.'
    The daughter: 'For petrol?'
    The father: 'A repair garage.'
    The daughter: 'For a repair?
    The father: 'No, for a spark plug.'
    The daughter: 'What's a spark plug?'
Never someone to pass up the opportunity of lecturing the digital generation on the subject of mechanical technology, I embarked on a long overview of the workings of the combustion engine, how the spark plug delivers an electri-

cally induced spark to a small amount of petrol, how the petrol explodes in the cylinder forcing the piston to move, how the movement of the piston is transferred to the drive shaft, how the rotation of the drive shaft is transferred to the wheels, and hey presto, the vehicle moves forward.

The daughter: 'What if it's in reverse?'

The father: 'Or backwards.'

The daughter: 'So why do we need a spark plug?'

The father: 'Because I'm writing a poem about one.'

As we turned into the yard in front of the garage I could sense the gears and cogs in her mind turning over and her imagination anticipating the impending collision of literature and engineering, a car crash which she would prefer not to be a part of. We opened a small wooden door cut into a larger wooden gate and stepped over the threshold. Inside it was chilly and dark, everything dripping with oil or coated in rust, and just the sound of a portable radio playing on a windowsill. Eventually a man in filthy blue overalls emerged from under the front wheels of a Volkswagen Passat, wiped his hands on his thighs and asked what he could 'do me for'. *Don't mention the P word*, I could feel my daughter thinking. *Please don't say the P word.* We followed him into a small office at the back where the shelves were stacked with log books, manuals and boxes of spare parts branded with famous names from the motor industry: Lucas, Michelin, Firestone, Dunlop, Ferodo, Bosch, Philips, Motul, STP.

The father: 'I'd like a spark plug, please.'

The mechanic: 'Just a spark plug?'

The father: 'Yes, please.'

The mechanic: 'What gauge?'

The father: 'Doesn't matter.'

The mechanic: 'They're not a standard fitting, you know.'

The father: 'Yes, I know. Don't worry. Any size will do.'

He rubbed his big black beard with his huge dirty hand, resting his backside on the metal desk, and even though I would have preferred not to humiliate my daughter, standing there in a small puddle of greasy water in her school shoes and pretending to look at something interesting on the floor, I knew that the inevitable moment of embarrassment was almost upon us.

'So what's it for?' asked the mechanic.

Don't do it, my daughter's body language was shouting, *Don't say the P word*, was her silent scream. But having come this far and being so close to getting what I wanted I had no option.

'For a poem,' I said.

In the dimly lit office, within the dark fuzzy circle of his beard and black curly hair I saw the mechanic's expression contort into the facial equivalent of a question mark, and even though she had turned towards the wall I knew for certain that my daughter's eyes were closed.

Here in Great Torrington, with the mic now mended and late-comers settled in their seats, I talk about how my dad worked in the car trade for several years, and during the early seventies would come home in a different vehicle almost every month, usually some old banger that he was doing up and would sell on for a small profit. And because I liked nothing better than to set off with him for the day in the passenger seat of his latest jalopy I grew familiar with the breakers' yards and scrapyards of the West Riding of Yorkshire. Cemeteries for the car industry, they were usually found at the arse end of town, behind the railway or near the canal. The gates would be open, and just inside the fence there'd be a Portakabin or shipping container that served as an office. Beyond that stood a shanty town of dinted metal and crazed windscreens, with shadowy avenues or ginnels between the lines of written-off Fords and Vauxhalls stacked three or four cars high. A tired Alsatian chained to a bumper and half asleep on a car roof might bark a couple of times, but otherwise those places were usually deserted, with no one around to answer questions or accept payment. In one such scrapyard in Queensbury, or Dewsbury, or Wakefield, or Elland, I unwittingly stood guard while my dad leaned into the open bonnet of a beige Hillman Imp, then began walking towards the exit at a pace that suggested we should skedaddle. Once inside our own car, and before releasing the handbrake and heading for home, he revealed the object of our mission, a spark plug, which he dangled in the air between us, pinched between his finger and thumb. If razzmatazz is discouraged at modern poetry readings, then props are also frowned upon. Nevertheless, on the stage of the Plough Arts Centre, Great Torrington, I produce a spark plug, the spark plug purchased from a Huddersfield repair garage much to my daughter's agonised embarrassment and which I just happen to have in my pocket, and talk the audience through the anatomy of this most intriguing device, beginning with the tip or nose at one end, down through the porcelain insulation, to the electrode at the bottom, a small gap across which a mini bolt of lightning is generated, the gap in which I saw the glint in my dad's eye as he held the stolen gizmo in front of his face that day. And the clinching detail, written in red capital letters around the cream-coloured case, the word 'CHAMPION'. Then I read my poem 'Prometheus'.

*

Back at the ranch it's so dark I have to grope my way along the fence until I feel the cold metal of the latch, then inch down the wooden steps towards the path, hoping Hern and Orla are no longer patrolling the grounds. A light appears on the porch, several small lights in fact. It's Simeon, doing his accounts at midnight, who has come to the door holding a silver candelabra to investigate the disturbance. We chat for a few minutes, but all I can see is his Cheshire Cat smile floating in mid-air and glimpses of the curly red locks of hair that frame his face. He offers me a drink but I'm knackered, all talked out, and missing home. He points to an indistinct place in the distant blackness of the lane where I might get a mobile-phone signal, but the line is dead. I feel as if I've already been away for weeks, and the night sky is a measure of how far I still have to travel, because I'm due to arrive in the Scillies on a full moon, and tonight the heavens hold a thousand stars but nothing bigger or brighter than a pinprick. After stumbling back to the cabin I go to bed with the thought of those two enormous hounds lying just centi- metres away from me through the partition wall, hearing them yawn and twitch, imagining their slack overlapping limbs and their smouldering body heat, eavesdropping on their dreams.

Instow to Westward Ho!

Wednesday 4 September

At seven thirty in the morning the whole encampment is dripping with dew, including my socks, now unwearable and hanging among the Tibetan prayer flags. In the early sun everything appears to be made of melting gold. Inside the cafe, from the other side of the counter and behind a wok, Simeon produces a fried breakfast out of a bowl of flames. I can see his face now because his lively, rust-coloured hair is scraped back and noosed with a scrunchie. As the writing on the side of his van indicates, as well as co-managing the Bunkhouse he has a day job as a landscape architect. He does a lot of playgrounds, he says, and has just been up in Somerset making a Viking longboat, for recreational or educational purposes I assume rather than for pillaging and raiding sorties along the coast of Wales or as a rescue craft the next time the Levels flood. We talk about bartering, skill swaps, crowd funding, the share economy, the Bristol pound, and the way the internet and eBay in particular (by accident more than design) has done more for recycling than most local or even national governments have ever achieved. Even the cabin we are standing in was once a chicken coop on a nearby farm, and began life as a seamen's dormitory in Plymouth.

There's a small group of people in various forms of walking attire milling around at the rendezvous point in Instow.

Oliver, who has collected me and is transporting the Galapagos Tortoise to his house near Westward Ho!, says they look like a bunch of strangers who are waiting for a poet but haven't been able to admit it to each other. Des and Clare are friends, so is Andrew. I don't know Ian but he's from Huddersfield, which is as much explanation as he offers and no more than I require, and he's brought Gerald, who will become the unofficial photographer for the day. The walk is pretty much a replica of yesterday, a long flat march along the side of the estuary on a tarmacked cycle path, a hairpin turn via another 'Long Bridge', this time in Bideford, then a stroll down the opposite sleeve of the inlet and out towards the coast. The tide is still draining away, exposing the usual inventory of fly-tipped items on the muddy river bed, including three or four bicycles and the inevitable shopping trolley. The large structure dominating the shoreline on the opposite bank is part of Appledore shipyard. Like most shipbuilding enterprises it has gone through periods of boom and bust, turning out all manner of boats in its lifetime, from survey vessels to dredgers, from luxury yachts to tall ships. It built the *Scillonian III*, described to me recently as a floating sick bucket, so that's something to look forward to, and when the big doors of the hangar are opened and sections of aircraft carrier are floated down river on pontoons, as they still are on occasions, it is, apparently, a sight to behold. Appledore itself smells of fish, which from an economic perspective must be a good thing, and the famous local ice cream, Hockings, tastes salty to me, as if the cows have been grazed on the sea marshes and dunes. There's a 'tidal bell' on the front, an art installation inscribed with a poem. The bell is activated by the rising waters and was designed to call out to other tidal bells along the shore, making the whole coastline chime and ring with news of the sea's return. It gives out a rich, sonorous and resounding dong when I climb onto the frame and manually swing it back and forth, although several people on the front look up as if I've sounded the nuclear alert, and a man opens an upstairs window in a house across the street and gives me a long hard stare. Irsha Street could be the set of *Under Milk Wood*, higgledy-piggledy terraced houses either side of the meandering lane with doors painted every colour of the rainbow and a few more besides. There are double yellow lines on both sides of the road even though there's barely room for a single vehicle to wiggle past the doorsteps and wheelie bins. At the lifeboat station, through the open doors of the building in which it's polished and cherished, the gleaming boat and all its shining accoutrements look like an exhibition in an art gallery or museum. Then the path steals in front of a row of cottages and across the rocky foreshore before heading out into Northam Burrows Country Park, a lesser version of Braunton Burrows on the other side of the estuary, made up of dunes and a low-lying coastal plain. The golf course here, the Royal North Devon, is said to be the oldest links course in England, and rumour has it that during a competition held at low tide every year members from this club attempt to drive onto the fairways of the Saunton course across the water, and vice versa. Another local custom is pot walloping, where school kids are cajoled into chucking all the washed-up pebbles and stones back onto the beach. There's a good environmental reason for returning the shingle to where it might best protect the crumbling land, but I suspect the Royal North Devon are the biggest winners in this arrangement; one of those stones would play havoc with the blade of a motorised mower, or bounce an otherwise respectable approach shot into an unplayable position, i.e. the waves. We picnic on the 8th tee, a 239-yard par three, and during a lull in play I substitute the flag on a nearby green with my holly stick and hat, and take a photograph. The conversation turns from golf to proper sport. Ian says that he worked for a while in local government on the Scillies, where just two football teams contested three competitions: two cup finals and a 'league'. The team he played for *did the treble* that year. As someone whose duties included the organising and overseeing of council and general elections he also remembers the difficulties of setting up polling stations and collecting ballot boxes in a constituency made up of several islands cut off from one another at certain periods of the day by the tide.

Untethered horses are grazing the scrub between here and the mainland. Gerald says that in the days before environmental consciousness this entire point was a landfill site, and storms or tidal surges often uncover layers of unsightly and embarrassing archaeological refuse from the way we used to live, including piles of asbestos. Tipper wagons and bin lorries were once a more common sight than the ice-cream vans and golf buggies that cruise the area these days. For the last couple of miles we venture onto the sand, the tide being so far out it looks like a mirage, then clamber onto the high shingle wall that forms a natural rampart all the way to Westward Ho!. Along the crest sunbathers and picnickers have dug out foxholes and emplacements to escape the wind and enjoy the view from an elevated and entrenched position. The noise of six pairs of feet clattering across the sliding, clinking stones makes it impossible to talk, almost impossible to walk, so the concrete slipway at the end comes as a relief both to the ears and the feet.

*

If the British seaside town is struggling to keep its head above water, and the independent book shop is finding it hard to stay afloat, and the publishing industry is swimming against the tide of electronic books and every other form of digital entertainment, then I have to take my fancy hat off to Walter Henry's independent bookshop in Bideford for a determination worthy of King Canute. I'd never come across the surname Chope before, but the Chope family who own the shop are well known in these parts as owners of the former department store, owners of the local haber-dashers ('dressmaking and craft supplies, wool and knitting accessories, curtain nets and voiles, fabrics and patterns, name tapes, cushion pads, gipsy tights, knitted cotton and thermal underwear . . .') and owners of the large car park at the back of the main street. We enter via a yard, a store-room, a lobby, several doors requiring several keys and a toy 'department', then go through to the long-by-narrow book-shop itself, where collapsible wooden chairs are arranged from front to back in rows of five or six and tea and biscuits are available on a trestle table at the rear. I'm reading in the window and stand by the front door as people arrive, like a pageboy at a wedding. One woman hands me her ticket, so I tear it in half, hand her the stub and invite her to help her-self to refreshments. From my notebook I read a new poem called 'Miniatures'. About the Redferns, our childless next-door neighbours when I was a boy, who became surrogate relatives and default babysitters to me and my sister, and were accorded the titles 'auntie' and 'uncle', though they were more like grandparents in outlook and age. When he wasn't working in the mill, Fred spent all of his time in the garden shed, or the 'hen run', or tunnelling under the house, digging out new cavities among the foundations where he stored his tools and worked his lathe. Elsie's life seemed to revolve around laundry. In some kind of cauldron in the cellar she'd boil-wash Fred's white shirts and their white bed sheets and pillowcases, then haul them up the stone steps and peg them on the washing line that hung between our gable end and theirs. Whenever I picture her, she's emerging through clouds of steam with her arms full of sodden, heavy cotton, hoisting the sagging washing line into the air with an extendable wooden prop, her face red and wet, her curly grey hair plastered flat to her head. If she wasn't doing the washing she was 'tatting', some arcane form of needlework or macramé by which she produced coasters or table mats out of knotted string, or even an anti-macassar given several years. A shop like Chope's Haber-dashers would have been a palace of glittering delights for Elsie. The Redferns were scrimpers and savers; they had put money aside to bring up a family, but when that family never materialised they seemed to have invested in expen-sive ornaments instead, Capodimonte figurines which I played with as toys, staging scenes and stories with the pout-ing princess or the mounted cavalier in the amphitheatre of their hearth. In some unconscious Freudian way I'd prob-ably cast those model characters in the roles of my parents, who'd left us next door to go out gallivanting or were put-

ting on plays and shows of their own in local theatres. I saw
the Redferns less and less as I grew up, and in some ways
deserted them. But I shared the same birthday as Elsie so
there was always an exchange of presents at the end of May,
together with a mild reprimand on their part, about how
they never saw me these days, and how I should stop being
a stranger. By my twenty-first, they'd heard how I'd fallen
under the influence of poetry, and wanted to give me a book
but had no idea where to begin, so I bought a copy of George
Mackay Brown's *Fishermen with Ploughs* and handed it to
them, then they handed it back, wrapped in brown paper,
tied with a length of gardening twine, with a fiver inside
which fell to the floor between us when I opened the covers.
I'd picked up *Fishermen with Ploughs* in a junk shop down
by the open market. Huddersfield's only recognised bookseller at the time was Greenhead's. The poetry section was
upstairs, a selection of about twenty titles, most of which I
went on to buy or read in the shop sitting on a portable 'step'
on casters, like an overturned bucket, for reaching up to the
top shelves. Huddersfield Lending Library had a wider
though bizarre poetry collection, or books could be ordered
via inter-library loan, arriving weeks or sometimes months
later, usually after the moment of need or desire had passed.
It was another age, a time of eclectic, eccentric and erratic
reading habits determined by a lack of choice, an era before
the internet offered access to everything, everywhere, any-
time, before online shopping made it possible to summon
obscure and even out-of-print poetic resources right to the
letter box, while simultaneously sucking the blood out of
shops like Walter Henry's. The mighty Amazon, both the
water of life and the river of death.

It's daunting to read in a bookshop, among so many books. Who writes all these things? Who reads them? How can a slim volume make itself seen or heard tucked away among the thousands of embossed titles, celebrity autobiographies and glossy hardbacks? But a kind of homecoming, and satisfying and humbling to articulate the written word in a room which appears to be constructed from books, whose very fabric and architecture is books, where the walls and furnishings are made from the covers or the spines of books. And the event is a success in the sense that the venue is as full as physically possible, that a few units of stock are sold and that I manage to speak above the noise of Bideford traffic. In fact by the end of the evening I have become practised in timing the pauses and stanza breaks to coincide with the sound of boy racers in their supercharged hot hatches or astride their over-torqued bikes drag-racing up and down the hill outside the shop. Today's walking party are going in search of a Wetherspoons for a reasonably priced pint and a value meal, but by ten o'clock on this trip all I want is a blanket and a pillow. In the back of the car the two Chope daughters are high on an overdose of shortbread and chocolate brownies, loud with chatter about packed lunches and clean shoes for their first day back at school tomorrow, and probably relieved to be able to speak again having endured the enforced reverence of the poetry reading. The Chope house is a large green and white semi on a quiet lane behind the marsh. I'm in the attic – the poet's room. There's a storage area under the eaves sectioned off with a gingham curtain, a hardback copy of Eric Newby's *What the Traveller Saw* on top of the bureau, and my pair of dew-soaked walking socks drip-drying in the shower.

Through the Velux window the pubs, bars and amusement arcades of Westward Ho! to the left are winking and flashing their salacious semaphore, and to the right a light buoy in the channel pulses meditatively on and off, on and off. But both the Skern – a maze of mudflats, brackish streams and grass-tufted banks – and the Burrows, where wild horses wandered and feral golfers strutted a few hours ago, have entirely disappeared, inked out by the night and erased by the tide. It's just blackness, with no visible horizon to divide the black of the land from the black of the sea, and the black of the sea from the black of the sky.

Westward Ho! to Clovelly

Thursday 5 September

Oliver drops me off in his sunset-red, left-hand-drive West-falia VW camper van. They don't build them any more but there's a guy who imports them by the container load from California, where they've lived long, easy-going, rust-free lives, untroubled by frost and road salt. Westward Ho! is a settlement conceived entirely around Charles Kingsley's lit-erary vision; I'm walking out of it as quickly as I walked into it, without making any investigation into whether its famous exclamation mark is either warranted or deserved, but that's the way it goes on this trip: sometimes I'm pitched into the heart of a community, sometimes I'm just passing through, and sometimes my feet barely touch the ground. The rendezvous point is the 'haunted house' at the west end of town, a dilapidated, gothic construction straight out of *Scooby Doo*, especially with Oliver's Mystery Machine parked near by. No one seems to know if it's occupied or abandoned, though on Halloween locals claim to have seen lights in the belfry and heard screams in the basement. I've progressed onto yet another map, though I won't need it today because Dave Edgecombe is here again to walk and talk. A former path warden, this is very much his patch, though at one point his loyalties were divided between a cricket team in Westward Ho! and a football team in Clovelly, and he once jogged this section there and back to be able to play for both clubs on the same day. 'Couldn't manage that any more,' he says, though he still strides along at a fair pace and never seems out of breath at the top of each deeply incised combe, of which there are several over the first three or four miles. The tide is about halfway out and still receding, revealing wave-cut platforms at the base of each cliff, those striated and furrowed bedding planes which from a distance appear to have been raked or ploughed. Inland the scenery has a 'Downs' appearance: rolling hills, farmed fields, managed hedgerows, country lanes, intermittent copses and the vague outline of what Dave thinks might have been a racecourse at one time, and it's not difficult to imagine thoroughbreds galloping along the gentle contours of that particular cantle of the landscape. Somewhere after Green Cliff I help myself to a three-berry elevenses, with a sloe for an appetiser plucked from an overhanging blackthorn, bitter green flesh beneath dry purple skin, then a handful of sour elderberries for the entrée and a fat juicy blackberry for dessert which tastes almost sweet by comparison. A few days ago I sat outside Geoffrey and Kirsty's graveside residence trying to mend my boots by applying epoxy resin with a wooden lolly stick, cobblers being in short supply in Swimbridge. The seams appeared to have stuck, but descents and climbs through Westacott Cliff and Portledge have reopened the pinch-points on both insteps, and the only other footwear I have with me is a pair of lightweight canvas trainers with soles so thin that if I tread on a penny I can tell if it's heads or tails.

Some of the inlets and valleys along here are privately owned and have a more managed, even artificial air about them, largely to do with the planting of game crops and brush to provide forage and cover for pheasants, which are reared in their thousands throughout the year then shooed into the flight paths of high-velocity buckshot. It's impossible to turn a corner or step over a stile without startling half a dozen of them into an exaggerated and extravagant escape. A pantomimic group of two females and several juveniles scuttle along in front of us for hundreds of yards, scrambling up steps and squeezing under gates before finally fleeing through a gap in a hedge and flapping away as if their tails were on fire. At the mouth of a stream we sit on a washed-up tree on the beach for a breath of air and a swig of water, and Dave eats his 'lunch', which is an energy bar pulled out of his back pocket. 'Not really a lunch sort of person,' he says through a mouthful of oats and sawdust. This section of the coast is a natural collection point for floating debris, to the extent that grey boulders and coloured buoys appear present in equal numbers. Some of the stones – about the size of bowling bowls – are patterned with streaks and stripes of brilliant white quartz. Dave once found one in the shape of an 8, which now sits outside his door announcing the number of his house. A little further along some enterprising and creative person has engineered a working hammock out of driftwood and washed-up nylon netting which supports all twelve and a half stone of me with ease, and Dave obliges with a photograph. The pink-orange sandstone protuberance in the cliffs at Peppercombe is an unexpected colour in the palate of the landscape, as is the little wooden cottage painted in the chocolate and cream livery of the Great Western Railway. Through the woods that follow we know we're the first visitors of the day because of the damp cobwebs that break with an

electrical tingle across our faces. They are delicate cats' cradles strung between oak trunks, some precious and golden where sunlight breaches the canopy and falls across the fine threads and intricate dew-jewelled designs, so tearing and slashing them with my big stick seems like a crude act of thuggery or desecration.

*

The tide rises and falls. The cliffs lift then drop. The hour hand of the sun arcs across the sky. The days come and go, so do the towns, villages and beaches, as do names and faces, bookshops, theatres, bunkhouses, back bedrooms and village halls. The miles pass. Slowly, but they do pass. And I press forward, each new step overtaking the last, and the earth rolls away underneath. It's a treadmill, this journey, or a roller coaster along the coast, or a motion picture with emphasis on the *motion*, a film that keeps spooling on from scene to scene. Or it's a book I'm reading or the book I'm writing, every day a new chapter, every word a footfall, the path like a sentence, a line of language always heading off into the distance. Even when I lie down and sleep the momentum carries me forward in images and ideas and dreams. Is that why it seems so shockingly silent and so abruptly still in this tiny, two-room dwelling on the edge of the land, where time feels to have stalled or even stopped? I start again from the front door, cataloguing the ephemera as I go, list-making, auditing the evidence of a deserted house and vacated lives. Each object feels like a clue: the sauce boat, the gravy boat, a bone-handled knife, a rusty cheese grater, an oil lantern, a hessian bag, a shoe brush, half a dozen earthenware bowls, a *Collins Dictionary*, a *Pears Cyclopaedia*, the Holy Bible, a packet of playing cards, a bottle of Harvey's Club Amontillado, a glass jar filled with shiny toffee wrappers: emerald, ruby, sapphire, diamond, gold. This brick-built one-up one-down construction on the seaward slope of Bucks Mills was a summer studio for artists Judith Ackland and Mary Stella Edwards, their 'Cabin', as they christened it, and very much a home from home going by the personal effects that line the shelves and fill the drawers. A painting by Edwards shows Ackland at work in the Cabin, and the pots and jugs on the wall behind her still occupy the same positions today, because even though the building speaks of a simple, contented lifestyle it was one that was to be dramatically interrupted. Or rather abandoned. Ackland died in 1971 and Edwards never returned, so everything here lies just as it did at the end of that last summer, as if awaiting a return. A folding chair hangs from a hook on the wall, as does a walking cane and a tattered brolly at the turn on the stairs. Brown linoleum lines the floor of the upper room. There's a corner washstand, a mirror, dried teasels in a vase, a tin of Dab-It-Off 'triple solvent' dry cleaner, a Band Aid tin, a jar of Maxwell House instant coffee, and a single bed with a white bedspread, although another bed pulls out from beneath it, and the curtain rail across the roof suggests that modesty and privacy were still required in this especially intimate setting. Most touchingly, in a cardboard box full of artists' brushes and paints there's a tiny pair of reading glasses with Judith Ackland's name written by hand on the inside of the case. The view from the side – a landscape of open sea and craggy coastline back towards Braunton Burrows – could have been one of Ackland's own paintings, caught and held in the flaking frame of the window. All of this in a building only fifteen floorboards wide. The polite coughing from below is Justin from the National Trust, who's come back to see me off the premises, put the long-shafted key back in the keyhole, seal up this cross-section of time and space, and leave Judith's and Mary's personal effects to the dust, the spiders and the years.

At the bottom of a path bolstered on the inland side by stacks of gabion cages crammed with crushed stone we eat a full lemon drizzle cake between the three of us and Dave tells the sad story of a young French trawlerman who drowned along this stretch of the coast sometime in the eighties. The shore is an untidy mess of loose boulders and jagged rock formations, including the Gore, a natural spit extending into the sea at a shallow angle like a sunken jetty or partly submerged runway and still visible as a dark and presumably dangerous reef a few hundred feet out. It was built by the Devil in an effort to construct a walkway between here and Lundy, but he abandoned the project when his shovel broke.

*

Today's walk is only eleven miles but it feels further. It might be because the physical effort is beginning to take its toll, or it might be to do with the continual ups and downs along the coastline that act as a constant impediment to forward advancement, or it might be a result of the woodland landscape that characterises the journey beyond Bucks Mills, with no real views and therefore little sense of progress in relation to more distant landmarks. Where the canopy does open up the sight is all ocean, silvery-blue and unlimited to the edge of the world, magisterially wide with no definition to its vast featureless form other than occasional stretch marks and creases across the surface where currents and wind have pulled in different directions. The path picks its way through oak woods shaggy with moss, and through the shady, crunchy understorey below lines of overgrown beech trees that were once hedgerows, and on into more woods where the greenness of the oak leaves and the greenness of the moss and the greenness of the bracken form a three-hundred-and-sixty-degree kaleidoscopic surround, broken eventually by the trademark pink-red trousers of the Honourable John Rous, onto whose land we have walked. Through a gap in the woods we look down onto the white-painted fishing village of Clovelly, of which John is owner and landlord. Other members of the welcoming party include Alison from AONB and her teenage son,

Scott, who twigged last night that he's studying my poems at school. Joy is here as well, who got in touch when she read that my itinerary brought me past her front door. Visitors to Clovelly are charged a controversial entrance fee and have to enter via the controversial visitors' centre at the top of the hill, but walkers on the Coast Path have free access via the long and stony Hobby Drive, a private 'road' which winds for a couple of miles across bridges and through wooded valleys. A tractor with some kind of suction device is spring-cleaning the track in anticipation of a shooting party, sucking up leaves, twigs and a fair proportion of the gravelled surface, then blowing the lot into the trees or the stream. Dave rolls his eyes: what happened to careful, accurate land management? What's wrong with a brush and shovel? Cinders eventually give way to cobbles and the famous old lane which slaloms down the narrow ravine past clusters of ancient cottages towards the sea. Sweating and short of breath, scarlet-faced tourists with cameras swinging around their necks are heading in the other direction. Two stoned-looking donkeys are drinking from a fountain dedicated to Queen Victoria; I'd like to stop for a photograph but the gradient and the momentum are hard to resist and a few minutes later we roll out onto the quayside, where a woman walks straight up to me and says, 'Simon, would you like to come mackerel fishing in my boat?' 'Not at the moment,' I say, as if in a minute or two I might change my mind, which I absolutely won't.

Joy points to a small craft rounding the pier and coming into the harbour, and to the man climbing out of it, unloading a pile of lobster pots, who then walks towards me in a woolly jumper and bright yellow wellies and shakes my hand. Stephen Perham is Clovelly harbourmaster and Clovelly's last herring fisherman and owner of the house where I'll be staying tonight. When I thank him for his hospitality he says, 'She invited you – I haven't got a clue who you are.' He plays the part of the salty, unapproachable sailor very well, though he's actually something of a personality around here and the go-to person when celebrity chefs and TV presenters make their way to this picture-book community, as they do often. Neither is Joy to be pigeon-holed or underestimated: once the local head case with a blue Mohican and a taste for cheap cider, she's now studying medicine and is on the crew of the Clovelly lifeboat, as is Stephen. A gang of small dogs are bouncing around their kitchen and our conversation bounces around the stone walls and the stone floor as Joy lifts a large pink crab from a pan of boiling water and says, 'Excuse me while I bash the shit out of this.' If I've eaten lobster before I don't remember, and surely I would have remembered. Served with the crab, boiled spuds, bread and butter and freshly squeezed lemons, it feels like we're eating the food of emperors. Stephen sets about sixty pots a day and considers one lobster from every six pots a decent strike rate. But there's barely any money it, he says, and bizarrely most of the shellfish is sold abroad. He's tactfully mute on the question of what it's like to live in a private community, where the rules and the rent are laid down by the big house at the top of the hill, but funnier on the subject of Clovelly as a tourist attraction. Many visitors think it's a kind of theme park with actors role-playing the parts of locals, and some knock at his house expecting a guided tour or a monologue from 'Crazy Kate', having confused the number on his door with the number on the tourist map. But as a sixth-generation Clovelly fisherman there must be something which keeps him here, and that something must be the sea, which appears to be his clock and his compass. In fact the whole house, once I'm pointed towards the spare room, is a shrine to the water: rowing pennants, paintings of harbours and ships, books about knots and boat-building, certificates, prizes, a pile of *Water Craft* magazines by the loo, a soap dish in the shape of a fish, and a pirate's chest in the crow's nest at the top. Looking out, for the first time on this trip the sea has taken on a bleaker aspect, more restless and shifting in its movements, colder and greyer in its manner, and by the time I've spruced myself up and gone downstairs Stephen has left the house to check on the boats. Watching him through the window Joy says, 'He doesn't go by the time, he goes by the tide.' Clovelly might look like a cute model village or a scene from a fairy story but the sea can be as cruel here as anywhere else. Earlier this year it smashed down their front door. When he comes back Stephen completes Dave's half-told tale about the French trawler. Having stayed behind in the hotel bar on Lundy, two crewmen decided to rejoin their trawler by borrowing a rowing boat, which was caught by the wind and the current and drifted away in the dark. One of the two managed to come ashore and raise the alarm at Bucks Mills. Lifeboats searched for the other man but without success. A fleet of French trawlers sailed up and down the Bristol Channel until they fished out his body several days later, a tragedy for the skipper of the boat not just because of the loss of a crew member but because that sailor was his son. Prompted by Joy, Stephen then describes how his own brother-in-law was lost, with another man, having gone out fishing in weather that worsened rapidly. Locals

gathered on the quayside expecting them back, and eventually the lifeboat was mobilised, with Stephen on board, and
the wreckage of the fishing boat was finally discovered to
the west. One body came ashore near Bude, the other on the
Welsh coast. A sombre mood has settled in the room now.
Even the dogs are quiet. I make my excuses and go for a
walk along the stony shoreline and behind the waterfall
where the wizard Merlin was born.

*

The reading, I readily admit, is not my finest hour, nor, I
imagine, Clovelly's greatest-ever occasion. The venue is the
Harbour Bar of the Red Lion Hotel, a sort of lower deck in
the open-plan side of the pub, when it might have been better to conduct proceedings in one of the smaller, self-
enclosed rooms at the back. To an audience of perhaps
twenty-five, Squire Rous, in his capacity as proprietor and
host, gives me a generous and valiant introduction, then settles down to my immediate right with a basket of chips.
Most people, I think, are here for the poems, including a
woman with a dog in her arms who I seem to have agitated
at the outset by reading an ill-chosen poem about a suicide.
She moves to an empty seat right in front of me and wants
to open up a conversation immediately, and when I ask if
we can save the questions until the end she disappears into
the other bar, only to reappear about ten minutes later
through the outside door, a manoeuvre which she completes
at least twice more before the end of the night. The hubbub
of the pub gets louder and louder the longer I go on. A bell
rings whenever a meal is ready to be served, the kind of

sharp, insistent ding-ding heard in a boxing ring to signal the end of a round or the beginning of the next, then a waiter appears with a plate in one hand and a set of napkin-wrapped cutlery in the other and circles the room trying to unite each dish with the person who ordered it. Whenever the door to the smaller bar opens, gales of gale-force laughter from people having a lot of fun come sweeping through. After about half an hour I haven't so much finished as simply faded into the background. John gallantly tours the room with the sock, and rather than watch the tenanted locals handing over money to the lord of the manor, or answer a morally complex enquiry from the woman with the little dog, I dive outside into the darkness and walk to the very end of the breakwater to phone home.

It's a blustery night. Stephen's house doesn't have a front garden, it has a harbour. In bed I listen to the clang of wires on masts and the heavy slapping of water against stone, but I must have slept well because over breakfast Joy tells me that her man was up three times in the night, like an anxious parent with a poorly child, to check the moorings and the ropes.

From Where I Stand

What is the sea?
        The sea is sleep.
Dog-headed fish and transparent
brine-blooded creatures loll and glide
in its depths. Boneless life forms
turn inside-out in its dreams but it sleeps.
Who is the sea?

A sleeper, asleep.
Hurricanes rake at its back, the full moon
drags it along by its hair, forked lightning
prongs at its flesh and it won't wake.
Not dead, then, not yet, but asleep.

When is the sea?
                    Whenever we sleep.
In the morning look back from the shore
at its sheets, wet with the piss and sweat
of the night, the tide at work laundering
sleep from its sleep with its sleep.

Where is the sea?
                    Wherever you sleep.
Walk to the edge where tired waves
snore on the shingle beach, leave
your wallet and phone on a rock, wade
up to your neck. Go under. Be sleep.

Why is the sea?
                    Because it sleeps.
Sleeps like a drunk, its feet on the pillow
of reefs and shallows, its head where light
never breaks, face down in the sand.
I know this. I know this, I am the land.

Clovelly to Hartland Quay

Friday 6 September

After the big daily mileages of last weekend I feel to be decelerating, even treading water. Eleven miles yesterday, ten and a half today, a mere eight tomorrow. If I'd been a bit more adventurous and less swayed by guidebook itineraries I might have nipped a couple of days out of the schedule, but there are certain stretches of the coast with no obvious place to stop or read, such as the leg between here and Hartland Quay, with only a snack van along the way. If I'd gone striding merrily forth last night it would have meant sleeping in a hedgerow and eating grass, and I'm no John Clare. Stephen and Joy drive me up the private, secret road out of Clovelly and transfer me into the custody of Kevin, with custody of the Galapagos Tortoise going to Kevin's wife Lesley, who will shunt it to today's destination. We set off past the big house, through a meadow where a herd of longhorn cattle are feasting on succulent wet grass and pay us no attention, and to one lookout point then another as the path makes a beeline for every natural pulpit or balcony of land overlooking the sea, then on past the 'Angel's Wings' – part pagoda, part village bandstand carved by a former estate butler when he wasn't decanting port or brushing dandruff from the shoulders of the aristocracy. The journey thereafter is through several miles of fields, most given over to pasture, plus a view and a whiff of one of Britain's controversial 'superfarms', with uncountable hundreds of black and white cows dotted around the site and a slurry pond so large it is rumoured to be poisoning the local water table. Kevin lives in Bristol and has a caravan not far from here in a village called Stoke. I've never met him before but after not very long I seem to know a great deal about him, from his entrepreneurial business dealings to his life of travelling. We begin in San Diego and Tahiti. A couple of hours later we're in Cape Town, then Easter Island. At some stage in the past (after a trip to Guadalajara or maybe Tijuana) he and Lesley opened the UK's first Mexican restaurant, which coincidentally was the venue for a crucial meeting between me and the woman who was to become my wife. As I tell him this I realise I have inserted him into the scene, and that from this moment onwards my recollection of that candlelit meal will always include an image of Kevin in a sombrero and poncho, humming 'Solamente Una Vez' while serving the refried beans and hard-shell tacos. In parallel with his CV and world-tour itinerary Kevin also has a long history of illnesses to narrate, including some particularly collectible conditions such as Lyme disease, Dengue fever, Bell's palsy and the spectacular-sounding Marcus Gunn jaw-winking syndrome. He invites me to look into his face for residual traces of those last two conditions but he looks fit and healthy to me. In exchange for the details of his medical history all I can offer him are a tonsillectomy when I was about nine and a more recent operation to remove polyps from my nasal cavities, a procedure overseen by one Dr Smelt.

While trading such sophisticated dialogue we have marched past several cliff faces above several inaccessible bays, past smugglers' caves, past the triangular Blackchurch

rock with its two side-fins like a warhead emerging from
the waves, past a heavily bearded raven blocking the path in
front of us like a nightclub bouncer, past a memorial stone
to a Wellington bomber which crashed into the sea here-
abouts during the Second World War, and past a fairy ring
in the grass, heading all the while towards the phallic-look-
ing radar station on the horizon with its rounded white
head on an erect concrete tube, arriving eventually at Hartland Point Kiosk, a green wooden snack shack with a cor-
rugated metal roof, lashed to the ground with steel hawsers
to prevent hurricanes flinging it into the next county. The
weather can be exceptionally punishing on this exposed
elbow of Devon, here where Atlantic depressions come
barrelling into the cliffs and where storm fronts that have
worked themselves into a frenzy over thousands of unim-
peded miles finally unleash their tantrums above the bare
land. The small heliport at the top of the road is often closed
due to high winds. Not long ago a bride and groom who'd
been helicoptered over to Lundy for a very special marriage
ceremony were stymied when the weather turned and the
rest of the wedding party became marooned on the mainland, including both sets of parents, guests, a band, the dress
and the ring. Only the vicar had travelled across with them,
the ultimate gooseberry, making awkward small talk with
the disappointed and frustrated couple.

Hartland Point with its lighthouse and rocky peninsula
is closed, by which I mean the track leading towards it is
gated and locked. Instead the coast path sweeps over the
headland and sets a new bearing for south, bringing with it
a dramatic change in scenery, probably the most dramatic
of the journey so far. The cliffs here are the product of

fierce geological processes and brutalising weather. Twisted and mangled seams and layers of rock form a towering, gruesome backdrop to every bay. Down at sea level, blackened formations run horizontally out into the water, each shallow platform rutted and fissured, as if some fantastical sea creature had raked its claws through the half-formed, half-set stone. At irregular intervals, groynes of crenulated and craggy stone form a series of gates or traps across each bay, raised serrated ridges like the tails of half-submerged crocs or dragons lazing at the sea's edge. Some of the darker and more crozzled sections of rock look like they were finished off with a blowtorch or born from a recent fire. Each new cove offers another theatrical staging of raw, naked stone, and at the foot of every sheer drop the debris and spoil from rockfall or landslip lies heaped and scattered, the high cliffs always succumbing to what W. H. Auden described as 'the pluck / and knock of the tide'. There's human residue as well: a metal boiler, the prow of a boat poking up through the floor of a sandy beach, and in the next bay a rusting anchor lying at forty-five degrees against a boulder, from a vessel of enormous beam and keel and impressive draught no doubt, but like a lapel pin from this distance and height. The path swerves and dips across Blagdon Cliff and Upright Cliff, playing hide-and-seek with the Cow and Calf rocks and peek-a-boo with Gull Rock, skirting the lip of Damehole Point, flirting with the cusp of Berry Cliff, before swooping down to Blackpool Mill then lifting and soaring across the open tract of the Warren, where the remaining archway of a ruined tower frames a stately home in the eye of its needle.

*

The first decision is choosing the right entrance. Am I 'Private' or am I 'Visitors and Coach Parties'? The second decision is choosing which door to knock at. There are dozens to pick from, though some on the front side of the house aren't real but painted on in *trompe l'œil* style. The third decision is choosing the correct form of address for the lady of the house, but this dilemma is resolved when I see a woman in a green and white striped pinny steadying the bottom of a stepladder, and when I ask her where I can find the owner she says, 'That's me. Angela.' We head off towards a cup of tea, leaving someone called Lofty rocking on the top rung with a light bulb in his hand.

Hartland Abbey was built in 1157 as a monastery. Like most country piles of its size and age it survives by opening its doors to the paying public. It's also available as a wedding

venue, hence the large marquee on the back lawn, the rum-
bling generator and three or four caterers carrying crockery
and cutlery from the house. Sir Hugh and Lady Angela
Stucley live here in the summer but not in the winter, when
it's impossibly cold and impractical to heat. Through a laby-
rinth of rooms, doors and period furniture we end up in a
modernised back kitchen, then I'm shown upstairs to my
chamber, a vast space with a high ceiling, complicated curtains, a basin in the corner and a four-poster bed. It's always
fascinating to peer behind the walls and through the windows of palaces and mansions, to see at first hand *how the
other half live*, though in many respects it's exactly as imagined, a combination of fabulous heirlooms, crumbling plas-
ter, priceless paintings, modified plumbing, organic wiring
and contemporary comforts. A bit like reports of the
Queen's sitting room, with a two-bar electric fire parked in
front of an antique fireplace and a jar of Ovaltine next to the
Teasmade. A corridor outside my room, partly roped off to
visitors and lined with the portraits of grand-looking ancestors, leads away into darkness and infinity. The bath under
the eaves is as narrow as the bed is wide, and I can't resist
speculating that the single strand of fairish hair in the bar of
soap came from the thinning pate of the future king of
England, who partied here during his last days as a single
man, so rumour has it. It's raining outside. Chucking it
down. A peacock drags its sodden robes behind it. Brown
sheep with black arses shelter under a tree. Water cascades
off the awnings of the marquee and along the leaded valley
gutter running beneath my window. Called down for something to eat in a small dining room opposite the family
kitchen I'm waited on hand and foot by Lady Angela, who

serves me with cottage pie followed by fruit crumble. I put a glass of red wine to my lips, the first alcoholic drink I've tasted since I set off, but after so long without booze it tastes more like Holy Communion than Pinot Noir and I push it aside. I'm sitting beneath a painting of William Stukely, 1687–1765, author of the *Itinerarium Curiosum*, a gazetteer of monuments and architectural designs, sketched and compiled during a tour of Britain. In the cellar of the house Lady Angela has put together an exhibition celebrating the intelligence and enquiring mind of the forebear who became a self-styled authority on Stonehenge, wrote learned papers on medical science and vulcanology, composed music for the flute and in later life was ordained as a vicar. His views, however, weren't always to be trusted; he once theorised that the centre of the Earth was made of water, and believed that elephants copulate face to face with the female animal lying on her back.

The Stucleys are not only my generous landlady and landlord for the night but with North Devon Coast AONB are also my gracious hosts for the reading, and have laid on a lavish buffet in the opulent dining room and filled the stately drawing room with chairs and settees around the focal point of the hearth. They're expecting fifty or sixty but a few have 'ratted'. To an audience whose attire ranges from printed T-shirts to tweed jackets and ties I read from my perch on the iron fender, with a pile of my books on a small drinks table inlaid with a wooden mosaic. It goes well: no bar meals being served, no extraneous hilarity, no inquisition from the floor and only one person asleep, a bearded gentleman on a sofa by the fire who stops snoring when his wife elbows him in the ribs. Among the usual repertoire I

throw in a few animal poems, about sheep, peacocks, ravens. And the adder poem, finished about an hour ago, prompted by Lady Angela telling me that they had just had a call from their holiday tenants in Blackpool Cottage, who'd 'flapped a bit when they found two snakes in the bath'. As part of the same conversation she also mentioned that one of her dogs, some kind of terrier who trots around behind her, is currently 'in the bad books' after attempting to eat a kitten. Later, a woman from the audience comes into my room, takes off her clothes and climbs into bed.

Hartland Quay to Morwenstow

8 MILES

Saturday 7 September

I've become very tired of picking up the guidebook only to read once again that today's stretch is considered by many to be the most challenging, most gruelling, most taxing, most arduous etc. etc. section of not only the north coast but the entire South West Coast Path blah blah blah. It's the kind of information that makes extricating myself from the sumptuous pillows and marshmallow mattress of a four-poster bed all the more difficult, especially when I have company. I'd met her on the path yesterday, just after Hartland Point. She was sitting at the bottom of a hill with her hood up – strange behaviour given how warm and bright it was at the time – and it wasn't until she peeled back the hood, took off her sunglasses and stood up that I recognised her as my wife.

Sir Hugh drives me down to the starting point at the Hartland Quay Hotel and has offered to escort me to the border of his domain a mile or so down the coast. I assume he's coming along as a courteous and informative guide as opposed to a landed gentleman keen to escort a roaming northerner off his land, though when I told him that the Galapagos Tortoise was so heavy because I'd filled it with his family silverware his response wasn't exactly one of amusement. A small crowd of walkers are waiting; rather than make a round of introductions I decide to pick them off en route, and we set off into the oncoming wind and the incoming rain. If the billing is to be believed, today is a story of two huts – not exactly blockbuster material. First, though, we pass through the remaining walls of a former swannery and then around the base of St Catherine's Tor, a conical, almost comical hill in the shape of a Walnut Whip but with a big bite taken out of the seaward side. The walnut, in the form of St Catherine's Chapel, is also missing, having come crashing down when half the mound slipped away into the water. Sir Hugh tells me that his ancestors once drove tractors and carts up a steep track to the summit, though it's hard to imagine how any wheeled vehicle could contend with such a gradient or understand what could be gained by getting to the top, apart from a good view. Land lost to the elements can't be retrieved, but other aspects of the coastline lost to changes in usage and management can. Sir Hugh is currently on a mission to reintroduce the large blue butterfly, *Phengaris arion*, which became extinct in Britain in 1979 but is making something of a comeback through dedicated conservation efforts. Its survival depends on a complex combination of environmental factors, including an abundance of wild thyme – its larval food plant – and the presence of a particular ant species, *Myrmica sabuleti*. As far as I can glean, at some point in the larval stage of its growth cycle the large blue tricks the ants into taking it underground to the nest, where it then feeds on ant larvae or mimics the embryonic ants and begs to be fed. Reintroducing the butterflies means reintroducing the ants, which means getting rid of the gorse under which nothing lives, which means bringing back sheep or goats or cattle to graze the slopes, then bringing back the rabbits which were taken out by myxomatosis introduced to protect crops. When I ask Sir Hugh what the large blue looks like, he says, 'Like the small blue, but bigger.'

Montbretia has colonised some of the streams. Natural England don't approve because it's non-native, but Sir Hugh doesn't mind it and neither do I. One species that he does object to, however, is ravens. They were here earlier in the summer and made such a din it could be heard from the Abbey, he says. It seems like an unreasonable prejudice, and also an unlikely story, but I keep nodding in agreement as he explains how his workmen have installed a height restrictor at the top of the track to keep them out, like heavy-duty goalposts and a crossbar, and only when he mentions that it took days to clear up the cans, bottles, needles and condoms do I realise that ravens aren't the source of his irritation, but ravers. By which time we've arrived at the waterfall at Speke's Mill, which marks the boundary of the Stucley estate. We shake hands and go our separate ways.

It's pouring down now. It feels as though a definitive change in the weather has occurred, as if the last page of summer has been turned and a new chapter has begun, under the heading of 'Autumn'. One of our group has led us along the exposed ridge of an 'alternative cliff-top route' and away from the shelter of the grassed valley running in parallel below. I think there are ten of us now but we've become a little bit fragmented along this arête. Rod refers to a big house on the horizon as 'the Dentist's house'.

'Is that derived from a folk tale of some kind?'

'No, it's just a big fuck-off house built by a dentist.'

The three teenage lads walking with him are his sons, I think, nonchalant in their trainers and jumpers, a kind of improvised redress to the rest of us in our elaborate and expensive walking gear. Rod and his family came down here from the Midlands after the birth of their youngest, when they realised they were living in a house with a brothel on one side and a crack den on the other. They came for the landscape and the lifestyle, and Rod talks with the authority and confidence (if not the accent) of a local, harking back nostalgically to the days when Concorde would pass overhead on its return from New York, using the radar beacon at Hartland Point as a marker and causing a thunderous boom as it decelerated and went subsonic. Others in the party are Bob and Yvonne, and Grant, and Mark. Mark and his wife were at the Red Lion in Clovelly and he has a more positive recollection of the event than I do, or perhaps a more charitable one. The past few years of their life seem to have been a big dipper along the peaks and troughs of finance and health, 'a bit like walking along this coastline'. He's telling me this as we scale the side of a formidably steep combe, and to keep cool he's unzipped the lower half of each trouser leg to form a pair of shorts, meaning that I'm eyeballing the red hairs and freckles on his lower calves for much of the ascent. Not only that, rather than removing them altogether he's left the detached rolled-down portion of each leg as a kind of ankle cuff, giving him the appearance of a shire horse with big shaggy hoofs.

'Not a good look,' I tell him.

'No, it's a winner,' he says, and offers me the entrepreneurial opportunity of 'getting in on the ground floor' for just a small investment and the promise of literary endorsement. Lunch is a carrier bag full of carrot batons and expensive cheeses, Lady Angela having over-catered by a factor of about ten for last night's buffet. A seal in the bay, the first one I've seen on this trip, bobs and rolls in the water like a big black turd.

*

The first hut is stone-built, restored, situated on the saddle of land between the Welcombe Valley and the Marsland Valley, and belonged to the poet Ronald Duncan. His daughter, Bryony, has come out to meet us, and I'm embarrassed to admit that I know very little about her father, other than what I've read in the guidebook. It isn't difficult to understand why he would come here to write, though such a dramatic view into the bay and across the ocean could prove more of a distraction than an inspiration. The hut functions partly as an unstaffed information centre, partly as a help-yourself library, partly as a picnic venue and partly as a literary shrine. The walls are decorated with Duncan's work, including the poem 'To Bryony'. Obliged to make a contribution, I scrawl a hurried haiku in the visitors' book, accompanied by an even hastier drawing. With her husband Andrew, Bryony invites us inland for a quick tour of their house and garden, a series of single cottages and glass-fronted studios on several levels connected by porches and stairwells and decorated with her pottery and his photographs. She doesn't even flinch as we wander among the fragile ceramics with bulky rucksacks and big boots. The quaint wooden bridge over the reed-clogged stream down by the valley mouth feels too modest to represent the border crossing between Devon and Cornwall, but there's a 'Kernow' sign on the other side, just before the steep climb to the headland. A different county, but more of the same ups and downs.

Hut number two also has a poetic history and was constructed by the Reverend Robert Hawker of this parish. 'Hawkers Hut' is reportedly the smallest 'property' in the National Trust's extensive and eclectic portfolio, being little more than a hidey-hole below the cliff top, accessed by a dog-leg of twenty or so steps. Dug into the soil bank and with a turf roof and a frontage made from ill-fitting driftwood and ship's timbers, it's like the entrance to an abandoned mine. Something of a 'character', the eccentric parson dressed in pirate boots and a yellow poncho, talked to birds, and would come to the hut to write verse and smoke opium. Tennyson was a visitor here on one occasion, though I can't find his name among those gouged into the wooden walls. Inside it's dank and earthy but snug, barrel-shaped at the back to accommodate the parson's ample frame, with a built-in bench to sit on and a little shelf attached to the lower half of the door to act as a desk. With the top half of the door open it's something of a kiosk, and the view alone would be worth selling tickets for. Hawker was a compassionate man as well as an oddball, showing kindness to animals, kindness to the unfortunate, and giving a Christian burial to bodies washed up along the coast. In the graveyard of Morwenstow Church a replica figurehead of the *Caledonia* watches over the graves of five of its crew, and inside the church Caledonia herself seems to hover in mid-air, the white-painted statue angelic but warlike at the same time with her sword and shield. In the out-of-focus, badly lit photograph that I take from below, her features have softened and her brightness has yellowed, reducing her to a fly-

ing, puffy-faced cook in a baker's hat with a pastry knife in one hand and a pie crust in the other.

*

If the water from my guest-room window looks soupy and sluggish in comparison to the feisty Atlantic it's because it's a river, not the sea, and if the breeze feels a couple of knots calmer and the temperature a couple of degrees warmer and the light a couple of watts brighter it's because I'm on the south coast. This walk might be about lacing the boot of Britain's south west peninsula but that doesn't mean I can't inspect the heel and the sole now and again. So from the Bush Inn in Morwenstow, Dorigen and Tony have spirited me between the rumps of Dartmoor and Bodmin to Danescombe Valley House, a former hotel with a veranda, a bar in the living room and the numbers still on the bedroom doors. I'm in room five, at the top of the house. Tony tells me that in its day the hotel had the pleasure of hosting Kenneth Tynan, John le Carré, one of the Redgraves and Sir Andrew Motion, who slept in *my* bed. It's hypnotic, up here on the second storey, on this cul-de-sac lane, at this wide crook on the River Tamar, watching the mud-brown water curl through its course between the treed slopes of Cotehele Estate on the right and a boggy water meadow on the left. I could be on a paddle steamer on the Mississippi, my eyes drawn to clumps of reeds and twigs being carried inland on the tidal push, on the syrupy, lazy, noiseless river with its viscous currents and slumbering flow. In slow motion a party of school children in yellow and orange fibre-glass kayaks come floating towards the house, the false screams and hysterical giggles of the helmeted, life-jacketed kids muted by the window pane, some of the kayaks facing backwards, others rotating in the stream, out of control but safe, knocking and bumping past the garden gate, herded by a guide who gives a push here and a prod there with his oar, drifting round the bend and out of sight, leaving the water to itself again and me to its quietness.

Tony wonders if I'd like a lift in the car to the venue, or if I'd like to 'stretch my legs'. Twenty minutes later we're still walking along the side of the river, past boatyards and moored cruisers, past a handful of swans, under a viaduct, then up the steps at the side of the building. Calstock Arts is a former Methodist chapel converted into an events venue and run entirely by volunteers. An enormous picture window provides a backdrop to the performance area on the upper floor, but the ground floor is still undergoing refurbishment. Up until fairly recently the building was home to publishing house Peterloo Poets, and according to Tony there are forty thousand unsold poetry books in the basement. They sell about thirty copies a month but are now having to think laterally about what to do with this unfortunate inheritance, which even Oxfam refuses to take. I jokingly suggest cavity insulation, to which Tony replies, 'Don't think we haven't tried it.' Even the authors don't seem interested in claiming copies of their own books, either to sell or to give away or to line the shelves of their studies. As poetry's representative in Calstock this evening I feel as if I should offer some explanation for the mausoleum of contemporary verse beneath our feet, or some solution to the problem of unwanted surplus stock, but just for a moment I seem to have lost my tongue.

Before the reading I wander out through a door at the back of the little office onto an outside balcony to gather my thoughts, check my flies are buttoned, rehearse an opening line and go through a few other little rituals in private. Except that when I turn around there are sixty or so seated people watching me through the giant window, as if I'm in a silent movie on the big screen. The opening line I've been working on turns out to be a bum note: when I announce that I don't think I have any words that could adequately compete with the darkening Devon landscape over my shoulder, about half the audience chorus, 'It's Cornwall.'

Walking back in the dark along the lane that runs parallel to the river feels like walking along the river itself. In bed I'm going back over the events and conversations of the day, Sir Hugh's voice still in my head with his quick speech and his clipped words, my mishearing of 'ravers' for 'ravens'. And that wry smile on his face as he described the life cycle of the large blue, its parasitic practices, how it inveigles its way into the home of a different species and scrounges food and shelter by pretending to be something it isn't. Was he really talking about butterflies?

Morwenstow to Widemouth Bay

Sunday 8 September

I first met James Crowden on a residential writing course in the early nineties. With his long sideburns, south-west accent, blue smock and muddy boots he looked like he'd fallen out of a Thomas Hardy novel. He arrived in a rusty old van which was full of sheep-shearing equipment and barrels of cider; with the back doors open it functioned as a pop-up bar for the week. Over glasses of cloudy, skull-busting apple juice he told me stories of his military background, of his walks across deserts, along frozen rivers and through mountain passes, of his time in hellholes and war zones, his tour-guiding in the Himalayas and backpacking in the Middle East, of his publishing history and his current employment on the farms and in the breweries of backwater Somerset. During those first few days I probably thought he was something of a Walter Mitty character, but over the years I have come to recognise that his life has been richer and stranger than most elaborate fantasists could convincingly describe. He even writes poetry, and why would anyone choose to lie about that? He's waiting near Morwenstow Church with his partner Carla, the two of them wrestling with coats and waterproofs in a blustery gale. All the way from Calstock the wind had shoulder-charged the car and the tyres had sizzled on the wet roads.

The first landmark of the day, after the aerobic workouts of Tidna Shute and Stanbury Valley, is the radar station

behind Lower Sharpnose Point. Swivel-headed security cameras scrutinise the grassed area between the perimeter fence and the radar dishes, of which there are about a dozen of various sizes, most with their antennae cupped to the east but one oriented to the west, decoding instructions from somewhere across the Atlantic no doubt. Tinged with shadow in this low light they are menacing, sinister structures in the landscape, a latter-day Stonehenge, and a mile or so later when I look over my shoulder they've rotated in our direction, seven or eight of them with their ears cocked towards our subversive and sarcastic conversation, the black pits of their eyes staring straight through us. A few shafts of sunshine strike diagonally at the surface of the sea but elsewhere there's *a lot of weather about this morning*, as James puts it, high-speed billowing grey and silver clouds flying right to left, the horizon ringed with darkness, the ocean looking heavy and chilly, the violent gusts along the cliff edge trying to bottle-top my hat from my head, Lundy still visible but as a dim smudge in the bottom corner of the frame, the rain horizontal and fast, each drop a tracer bullet fizzing past or pinging the side of the face. For the first time the handle of my holly stick is slimy to the touch, the bone-hard, bone-dry wood suddenly acquiescing to the elements, its tight grain turning to oil. No sooner is one combe conquered and the lactic acid in the muscles dispersed than another one opens its maw, and in we fall. At the bottom of Duckpool two camper vans are jittering in the wind. In between them, one very concerning individual wearing combat fatigues sits with his legs crossed and arms folded in the open door of his one-man tent, a vicious expression on his face, a black aura above his head, not to be approached. At the interface of land and sea the geology seems to have softened a little, being less exaggerated and contrived than it was around Hartland Point, though the coastline along this section is reputedly as treacherous as any, a notorious grave-yard of shipwrecks and drownings. Jan and Jackie are waiting on the next headland. They've walked out from Bude to meet us with promises of better weather ahead and a flatter route. We're approached by another couple who aren't looking for us but would like to know how far it is to the Hartland Quay Hotel, where they might stop for a bit of lunch. I don't think they believe me when I tell them it's a day and a half, because they carry on regardless, honey-mooners in inappropriate clothing, his T-shirt stuck to his chest with rain and already transparent, her skin-tight woolly jumper pearled with raindrops, the two of them cocooned in their own little weatherproof capsule of new love, their jeans sodden and their trainers ruined, their hands together and their fingers interlocked.

Another combe: another plummet then another moun-
tain-climbing expedition up the far side, and an especially
splashy one, because rain has accumulated behind each
wooden step, so it's like walking up through a series of sinks
or troughs full to the brim with water. Also, the tread–riser
ratio seems to have been designed at a very annoying one
and a half strides, making it impossible for anyone who isn't
a stilt-walker or a toddler to get any kind of rhythm going.
At Northcott Mouth a pair of lifeguards are setting up their
pitch, striding out onto the sand below with big yellow and
red flags, as if preparing for a medieval pageant or joust.
The only other people around are two men selling membership of the National Trust from the shelter of their National
Trust Land Rover, and I suspect they will have an unprofitable day. From up here there's a wonderfully vivid contrast
between the lush green of the wet grass in the fields to the
left and the giraffe-skin patterning of the wet sand to the
right, the path between them like a torn strip down the page
of a glossy magazine. And a last backward glance catches
the radar station in a rare patch of half-decent weather, wet
sunlight divesting them of their malevolence, giving the
white dishes the look of cereal bowls in a drying rack after
the washing-up. With the tide out we take the direct line to
Bude across the beach, and it's exhilarating to descend from
the promenade of the land and to be down at sea level again,
to see the undercarriages of the cliffs, their workings and
faults, all the caverns, caves, collapsings, columns, slabs and
fissures. In addition to which, there's a childish pleasure to
be had in breaking the rules, straying from the designated
route and choosing instead a course across the broad
cleansed beach, puzzling for bridges and causeways between

channels, tributaries and landlocked puddles of water as the last of the tide still drains towards the distant sea. Carla dematerialises at Bude, taking my Sue with her, so for the rest of the day it's just me and Royal Engineer-cum-pomologist Crowden, drying off in a Bude cafe, balancing along the lip of Bude lido, paddling through the mouth of Bude harbour, finding a fording place across the Bude canal, then leaving Bude to the bucket-and-spade brigade and the Sunday drivers, heading due south. We take a break on a bench by a couple of retirement bungalows near Upton. James fishes an apple out of his bag, a Miller's Seedling, apparently, picked from his own garden this morning, and talks me through the uses and qualities of this particular variety. Now doesn't seem the right time to tell him that I don't like apples, so I just keep polishing it on my sleeve for as long as his citation lasts, and fall back about ten yards when we set off so I can push it into a side pocket of my rucksack and smuggle two fingers of KitKat into my mouth. I'll give it to a horse, I think, though I'm not overly keen on horses either. Widemouth Bay is our destination. If there's an actual community it's hidden behind the hill, because here on the coast it's just cafes, surf shacks, public conveniences and car parks. Like life forms from another planet we seem to be the only people not wearing black rubber onesies, though James is more alien than me because when he peels off his waterproof coat he's dressed as Gabriel Oak.

*

It is typical of this journey that one minute I'll be climbing into the car of a complete stranger and the next I'll be up to my chin in their bath making merry with their soaps and products. Claire picks me up in a Chrysler Cruiser littered with crumbled plasterboard and brick dust and we head inland towards their half-converted watermill, which she describes as 'more of a work in progress than *Grand Designs*'. I'm billeted in the 'cottage' round the back, a self-contained former stable once occupied by a horse called Jip and a horse called Lion, according to an ancient diary written by the original miller. Claire explains that the toilet works but the shower doesn't. 'We would have fixed it if you'd been John Hegley,' she says. Which is why I'm soaking in the cast-iron tub off their master bedroom, listening to a digital radio in the shape of a Makita generator and helping myself to Vosene anti-dandruff shampoo. There are dozens of kids' bath toys lined up along the rim, plus a tube of electric lights running dangerously close to the water. With wet hair I set off for a tour of the property, beginning with the garden and grounds. Claire says I should count myself lucky that I'm not sleeping in the Pod, some sort of white plastic caravanette used as a playhouse by the kids and probably big enough to accommodate one adult, but only in the prone position, though unlike the cottage it does look sealed and mouse-proof. Across the lawn there's a shed made out of straw bales, and a pond they didn't know existed until they'd been here about six months and one of the kids 'discovered' it. Beyond which, wild and overgrown land extends as far as the vanishing point. Ben leads me along a winding path, overlooked on one side by a white mannequin in the trees staring in my direction. Further on we encounter the Chair of Chat, three dining chairs nailed to the three stumps of a felled goat willow, the seats raised into the air like somewhere a triumvirate of elves might meet in council, and for a worrying moment I wonder if I'm expected to sit there myself being bright and illuminating as I read my poems. Inside the mill it's part home, part industrial museum. Rooms with ceilings seem to have no walls, and rooms with walls seem to have no ceilings. The middle floor is overrun by children in a variety of fairy-tale outfits who are too busy with their make-believe to be distracted by me, and the ground floor is dominated by the immense and fearful-looking internal mechanics of the milling process, not least the colossal iron wheel, with many other toothed cogs and axles extending from it, plus gears and ratchets and the great circular grinding stone. Half of the big wheel is housed in a deep pit; looking down into it I can see lost toys, pieces of Lego and children's drawings. In a public building such a treacherous void would be roped off or glazed over for reasons of health and safety, but here in this kitchen it's an accepted feature, a place between the table and the stove. There are six of us eating, just the adults, the kids having been settled on a beanbag in the room over our heads, in front of a projector TV and a pull-down screen. At one stage a snooker ball drops past the dinner party, narrowly missing one man's bald head, which in billiard terms would have been classed as a cannon had it connected. Claire and Ben produce a proper roast meal from the oven, and it's comforting to be sitting down in a family environment with hot food and warm people. 'I met a poet in Canada once,' says one of the guests. 'It might have been me – I've been to Canada,' I say. 'No,' she says, 'I slept with him, so I would have remembered.' The group being a combination of long-term natives and immigrants from other regions of the UK,

conversation around the circular table turns to the social
complexion and psychological outlook of the south-west:
about the determination of small communities to stick
together; about holiday-home settlements like Port Isaac
which are ghost towns in winter; about attitudes to multi-
culturalism in this neck of the woods; about a Cornish tendency to see Cornishness as a kind of fame; about the line
between independence and isolation; about the Cornish language; about economic indicators in what is often referred
to as 'the poorest county in England'; and about Cornish
craftsmanship, which Ben says is second to none, even if
tradespeople are prone to disappear for a few hours when
the sun is shining and the surf is up. Out comes a big dish of
pudding, and I share a non-alcoholic beer with a man who's
off the booze after a blood clot in his leg. There's no mention of any poetry reading and I'm not in any rush to bring
the subject up, so by nine o'clock when the adults are scooping up their tired kids and bundling them into cars, I realise
I've had the night off. Later, Claire sits with her legs crossed
stitching name tags into school dresses and cardigans ready
for the start of the new term, and Ben tells me about his
research into air pollution. Back in the stable I check under
the bed for Lion or Jip, wedge the Galapagos Tortoise in
front of the large hole in the door to stop any night-foraging
species such as badger or wild boar coming in during the
small hours, and fall asleep over *An Illustrated History of
Combine Harvesters.*

Widemouth Bay to Boscastle

Monday 9 September

I don't know why I want to take a photograph of Claire's bath towels on the washing line in the garden, drip-drying in the morning dew. Art, is it? The pink one next to the turquoise one, and the little tin bucket full of pegs hanging next to them. Claire doesn't know either. 'Not bringing them in at night, makes me look all slutty,' she says. To compensate for last night's lack of a recital Ben and Claire wonder if I could read a poem for the kids before they go off to school. Trying to tap into the current zeitgeist of wizards and magic I read the scene from *Sir Gawain and the Green Knight* in which callow young Gawain decapitates the Green Knight, then watches in disbelief as the Green Knight picks up his head from the floor and puts it back on his shoulders. Behind her glasses, Bea's eyes get wider and wider, but Mirabelle, the younger of the two, slides down from her chair and seeks refuge behind her mother's skirt. The poem took me several years to translate, and during that time my own daughter kept asking me to tell her the story, especially the beheading scene, which she thought was hilarious. One day the published book dropped through the letter box and she asked me to read it as her story that night. Sitting next to her bed I launched into the opening stanza, but after about ten lines she yawned and said, 'That's enough, Daddy. Can we have some Clarice Bean now?'

*

Today feels like a fresh start, as if the slate has been wiped clean or the reset button pressed. I think it's because I'm alone, and so determined to stay alone that I sneak around the back of the cafe toilets at Widemouth Bay to avoid any would-be walking companions loitering in the car park, then canter along the first stretch of path with my head down and hood up. It's a chance to internalise and contemplate rather than broadcast and share, a day to witness and observe. To watch two surfers in the water, one litter-picker on the beach, a man in a business suit and laminated name badge walking two flat-faced pugs through the dunes, both dogs wearing navy-blue quilted gilets and harnessed with a set of reins. A day to note the colour palette of the open water – turquoise, jade, petrol, indigo, teal – and to convince myself that I'm finally tuning in to the nuances of the sea and the language of the coast. To think in poetic terms for a few hours, to begin writing a poem perhaps before suddenly recalling the forty thousand unsold books mouldering in the crypt of the former Calstock Old Chapel, a tomb of verse. And to realise that I'm developing an asymmetrical tan, my left arm and hand noticeably browner than the right from walking diagonally towards the sun's parabola. A drab-coloured dunnock hops away below a fence and there's a wren squirting about at ankle height in the undergrowth. At Wanson Mouth the path crosses a low bridge which is presumably a ford in times of greater rainfall, then wiggles and winds through a copse of straggly willow and small, scrubby oak. With every passing day along this peninsula I get the impression that the trees are thinning out, having to work much harder to achieve any

kind of status or standing, and my holly stick feels compara-
tively taller, straighter and prouder through every mile. The
rising, crumbling cliffs and the narrowing verge force the
path onto the road on a steep uphill bend around an outdoor
activity centre; in the absence of an instructor preaching the
Countryside Code a handful of kids with branded clothes,
city accents and urban vocabularies are playing dodgeball
with someone's rucksack. In the lay-by at the top of the hill a
couple (I think there are only two of them) are having sex in
the reclined passenger seat of a Fiat Punto. It's bright and
clear today but across the ocean individual clouds are hauling
their shadows and drawing their veils of rainfall towards the
shore, some destined to make landfall further south but others with my name on them no doubt, on a collision course
with my anticipated position on the path. Knowing when to
ferret out the elasticated over-trousers from the bottom of the
rucksack has become a bit of an art form. Too early means

overheating in their boil-in-a-bag confinement, too late means wet legs for the rest of the day. On this occasion I time it to perfection, sitting down on a bench to clad myself in water-resistant fabrics just before the heavens release their payload. The bench is dedicated to one Mervyn Northcott: 'No one truly leaves this place who loved it so', the inscription reads, which strikes me as both a testimony and a threat. Wet, spidery, exposed tree roots that vein the path are either a trip hazard or a slip hazard and to be carefully watched and avoided. Elsewhere the ground underfoot is a gummy paste of soil and rain, sticky and slimy along some sections and untrustworthy when heading downhill into the next combe, and the next, and the next. On a day like today I've no doubt that this is a more tiring and perhaps tiresome journey than the Pennine Way. Every valley crossing saps blood from the limbs and air from the lungs, and going up and down the gears all the time makes it impossible to build up any kind of momentum or to fall into a stride. Even on the plateaus the eyes can't stray too far from the narrow ribbon of the path because electric fences patrol one side and a fatal fall waits on the other. Not ideal territory for someone who likes to let his boots and his mind wander, not ideal for the daydreamer or stargazer or anyone who prefers to gawp at the horizon rather than stare at the earth. Looking means stopping, and stopping means having to start again, with all the associated wear and tear on body and soul that acceleration and deceleration demands. There's no cruising, no soaring, and definitely no coasting to be had here.

An area of flower-covered hillside to the right looks more inviting and interesting than a track through the fields, but signs erected by Cornwall Council explain the importance of steering clear of dangerous rocks, the expense of maintaining a right of way, and thank landowners for their ongoing co-operation. Lower Tresmorn is a nasty and dark incision, treacherous and vertiginous on the descent, unfeasibly steep on the other side, like a climbing wall where handholds and things to grab hold of are just as important as somewhere to plant the feet. Added to which, four mean-looking horses are straddling the re-routed path, two greys, one chestnut and a white, forcing me towards the scree and rubble at the cliff edge, where the original route has been cordoned off with orange plastic mesh and a skull and crossbones sign. At Cleave the route follows the absolute apex of the steep-sided valley, like a tightrope or airstrip leading nowhere but the blue horizon. Just when the path threatens to launch into mid-air it veers left at the very last moment then zigzags its way down the nose of the headland to where a herd of cows have blockaded the wooden bridge. Mushing and shooing has no effect, but remembering the last thing my dad said to me as I got out of the car I raise my holly stick with a biblical theatricality and a way opens up between the haunches and the horns. The several houses and cafes huddling in a cove between two all-engulfing cliffs are Crackington Haven. The open, widening beach of the same name is populated by a dozen or so dog-walkers and day trippers, with the silhouettes of surfers just about visible on the distant tide, thin black figures that stand upright on the hazy surface of the water for a few wobbling and miraculous moments before being subsumed into the ocean. After which it's another hill start into high, rolling scenery reminiscent of Lakeland fells, with fern-covered hillsides extending right down to the shore and the path looping past the natural archway of

Northern Door, through minefields of rabbit burrows and as far as High Cliff, which requires no description other than that provided by its name. On several occasions Boscastle is within sight and seemingly within easy reach, only for another cleft or bay to intervene, the final test being an adverse camber around the bulge of Hillsborough where the path is little more than a monorail following the outswinging contour of the land across a grassy slope that acts as prelude to a vertical drop.

*

On Monday 16 August 2004, even though weather conditions were relatively benign on other stretches of the Cornish coast, a dark reservoir of a cloud anchored itself over the catchment area above Boscastle and remained there until the narrow ravine that funnels through the town and into the pinched harbour was a biblical deluge that swept away trees, caravans, bridges and houses. So if today's Boscastle has the occasional appearance of a Cornish fishing village theme park it's because several aspects of it have been remade in its antediluvian image, recently built structures imitating original and eccentric architecture, with (presumably, hopefully) modern reinforcement and high-tech drainage behind the outward-facing local materials and traditional styles. It's impossible to imagine the force and fury of such a tumult on a day like today when the tide is out of sight and mind beyond the dog-leg of the cove and the river bisecting the valley is little more than a stream, barely a puddle in fact, which several ducklings are crossing on foot. Sitting alongside the channel the reinstated Youth Hostel looks both solid and comfortable. I was offered a bed there, but had already opted for a less conventional form of accommodation, which is why I am now standing in the foyer of one of Boscastle's most notable tourist attractions waiting for the manager. The woman behind the counter with the long white hair offers me a cup of tea but has to turn her attention to a couple of young Goths buying a medium-sized pentangle T-shirt and a bottle of Four Thieves Vinegar.

'Would you like those in a bag?'

I'm examining the ducking stool when Graham arrives and leads me to the upstairs flat via an external staircase.

*

Boscastle's Museum of Witchcraft doesn't usually do bed and breakfast, but many moons ago Graham was attempting to pitch his tent in fading light on a wind-swept headland, and having watched him wrestle with the flaps and ropes for an hour or so a local farmer offered him use of his hayloft for the night. Graham bedded down among the bales of straw, promising that one day he would pass on the kindness to a traveller in need of shelter, and I am the recipient of that good deed.

'Karma,' I say.

'Precisely,' confirms Graham.

We pass through an office with windows looking out onto the water, then into a library crammed with over three thousand books related to witchcraft and the occult. I can help myself, Graham says, if I fancy any bedtime reading, and he shows me how to 'borrow' a book by means of a blue plastic strip which must be inserted at the position from where an item has been taken and to where it must be returned. The 'flat' itself is through the back of the library, up a half set of stairs, and having pointed out the kitchen and bathroom and given me a key for the door Graham wishes me well and leaves me to 'make myself at home'. There's a wetsuit suspended from a wire hanger in front of the French windows, like a hollowed-out body. Other objects dangling from the beams include a plastic skeleton, a dream catcher and the outstretched wing of a bird of prey. Back in the library I run my eye across the shelves, following the carefully ordered sections through Witchcraft for Men, Witchcraft for Women, Witchcraft for Young People, Equipment, Persecutions, Green Man, Greek Myth, Superstitions, Birth Energies, and onward towards Astrology and the collected Harry Potter series. The 30-inch JVC TV and Toshiba DVD player in the corner break the spell somewhat, though on another wall there's a collection of slasher and vampire films that would sit comfortably in the bedroom of any moody adolescent or aspiring serial killer. And pentangles everywhere, several hanging from the ceiling, one painted in the soap dish next to the sink and one embossed on the leather cover of a 'coffee table' book of spells. I have a note in my itinerary saying, 'Graham isn't really into poetry,' and I can't decide if the two Kipling collections in the loo confirm or contradict that statement. Other bath-time reading matter ranges from *Bob Copper's Country Ways* to a publication called *Bollocks to Alton Towers*. Looking for coffee I find a jar of unspecified brown powder at the back of the kitchen cupboard but decide not to make a drink with it in case it's the granulated remains of Aleister Crowley or the charred bones of a heretic. Up the road I'm the only customer in the Old Manor House, 5.15 p.m. being too late for lunch and too early for dinner but the necessary hour for post-walk, pre-poetry-reading sustenance. Holidaymakers peer at me through the window as though I'm the proprietor having his private meal before the restaurant opens its doors to the public. On the radio an *X Factor* hopeful over-emotes a cover version of Cherry Ghost's 'People Help the People': 'And if you're homesick, give me your hand and I'll hold it.'

*

Burning torches light the way down the long drive to Wooda Farm, where audience members are already being served wine and beer around a glowing brazier. Janey, Ellen and friends cooked up the idea of this gig and there is a promise of puddings to follow. The venue appears to be some kind of private theatre or recording studio made of glass and wood, built in the grounds of a traditional farmhouse. Max, the owner, takes me into the space, a wedge-shaped 'auditorium' with adjustable and collapsible raked seating, an unexpected and ingenious architectural wonder in the middle of a Cornish field, a sort of ship-in-a-bottle building which at the end of the night might fold away into something the size of a matchbox. Everything is transparent, even the outer wall of the toilet, which faces a bank of earth, so visitors to the loo can sit and watch worms and bugs in the cross-section of soil beside them. I won't need a microphone, Max says, because it's purpose-built for acoustic performance, and there's a big armchair on the 'stage' in case I'd prefer to sit down.

'Do you prefer to stand or sit down?'

'I prefer to stand, but I think I'll sit down.'

'Oh, why's that?'

'Because I'm . . .'

'Knackered,' says another man, sticking his head into the conversation. 'He's fucked.'

*

The audience are a steep bank of fifty-some faces, with Max sitting proprietorially at the very back and the very top in the hatch of a control room or office, like a barn owl in its roost. Afterwards, someone warns me that, yet again, tomorrow is the hardest day's walk of the whole journey, then I'm driven back across black fields and down the black gullet of the valley into the dark village. In the flat there are no curtains and there's no phone signal. Cleaning my teeth, I half expect to look in the mirror and see fangs. Or see no reflection at all. It's midnight. There's an unlocked door in the corridor which I hadn't noticed before, not a broom cupboard but an entrance into the museum. So if I were minded to I could step inside and wander at will between the beeswax effigies lying in their carved sarcophagi and the poppet dolls stitched with real pubic hair and the phallic tusks, handcuffs, shackles, cauldrons and mounted skulls. Or I could prop my unbreakable and unshakable holly stick under the door handle and wedge it shut.

Boscastle to Port Isaac

Tuesday 10 September

It's hardly the crack of dawn but at 8 a.m. Boscastle is like an empty film set before the actors and crew have turned up. Even the water in the harbour looks dozy and slack, not properly awake. I walk past a high wall of stacked lobster pots and half a dozen fishing boats under the pier, then follow the path as it banks upwards onto the next headland, leaving the village asleep and the thin tapered valley yet to have its first drink of morning light. It's bright and blowy up on the tops but the elevation and exhilaration are short-lived because a Dantean descent awaits, a plummet into the grim and inhospitable gorge of Rocky Valley, just below Trethevy. Deprived of sunlight by its angle to the sky it's formed of iron-like stone, a fused and choked geology with a wild sea thrashing around in its dark mouth, pagan and primitive in a way that the ancients must have found irresistibly significant. So to enter its throat and to exit up the chimney of steps is to have *come through* and escaped. A family of five are helping an old man, unsteady on his feet, down the rocky path on the far side and leading him towards the edge of a stony promontory above a swirling pool. A great act of kindness is probably taking place, an elderly widower visiting the site of some romantic encounter, supported and steadied by friends and loved ones. Equally, they could be about to sacrifice him to the sea.

Say it quietly but King Arthur never existed. The most
that can be argued is a gap or absence in the circumstances
of these islands into which a sixth-century Arthur-like leader might fit, but as far as the historical record is concerned
there was no such person and no such king. And say it even
more quietly, but the Arthur that comes to mind when we
conjure up a chivalrous and fearless monarch surrounded
by loyal knights is as much a French invention as a British
one. The legend of Arthur might have sprung from the
deep roots of Welsh folklore but such is his power and
appeal that his character has been appropriated over and
over again by invading forces and dominant cultures, with
every writer and teller of Arthur's story adding their own
narratives and dress codes to suit a readership or audience
keen to believe in a single defiant and uniting figure, a 'once
and future king' who will rise again from the grave to
defend his people in their hour of need. Not that there's
much evidence of a French or Norman Arthur in the gift
shop at Tintagel Castle. Many of the action figures and
accompanying accessories are draped in the black and white
of St Piran or the flag of St George, or sport a variety of
heraldic devices, mostly crowns but one emblazoned with
three lions, because at a subconscious level the position of
captain of the England football team is yet another of
Arthur's allotted roles. I decide against buying a ceremonial
sword or a plastic breastplate, but chat for ten minutes with
a man from Halifax who has recognised me from a docu-
mentary I made about Arthurian Britain and wants to know
why it included footage of a non-league, mid-table fixture
between Ossett Albion and Prescot Cables. 'I can't remember' is the honest answer – something to do with language

perhaps or northern versions of the Arthur legend – though I have a much clearer memory of my stay in the Camelot Castle Hotel, the fortress-style pile that dominates the coast-line and the town of Tintagel as if it were Camelot itself. On the first night, a group of French visitors in Guinevere dresses and Lancelot capes were performing an elaborate dance ritual in the main lobby which culminated in a mass hugging session and a bacchanalian banquet glimpsed through half-opened doors at the end of a corridor. On the second night the owner or manager of the hotel sat me down in a big armchair in front of an open fire, put a complimentary drink in my hand and began talking to me about higher consciousness, eternal life and a kind of intellectual energy that would soon be rolled out among privileged members of the human race in a few years' time. I was high on Lemsip at the time; in combination with the free malt whisky it had rendered me incapable of anything other than a slow nodding movement, which my host must have taken as a sign of interest or consent. Later that night there was a shuffling noise outside my room and I watched as a leaflet containing introductory material was posted under the door. By that time I had a temperature approaching spontaneous-combustion levels and was slipping in and out of hallucinations courtesy of the paracetamol, the booze and a bottle of Night Nurse I'd been swigging from. I don't think I signed the forms or entered my credit-card number, and if I did subscribe to the Church of Scientology during those hazy, drug-fuelled, dream-filled hours, then I'm yet to experience any obvious benefits of membership, spiritually or otherwise.

It's about half nine when I walk directly below the hotel, keeping a low profile. A girl in the wooden ticket hut at

Tintagel Castle is waiting for her first visitors of the day, and several are on their way, either waddling down the tarmacked road or being brought to the toll bridge by Land Rover, all heading for the *Castel Dintagel* experience. I don't need to see King Arthur's 'birthplace' again, and opt instead for a vended take-away cappuccino from the English Heritage cafe before following the prescribed Coast Path route where it skirts around the stone-and-mud back wall of the fortification, then on towards the spectacularly positioned Tintagel Youth Hostel, built into a ledge above the cliffs at the end of a remote track, with an uninterrupted view of the Atlantic and a spillway of shale or broken slate to one side that on a dark or drunken night could easily sidetrack the careless walker and deposit them in the sea. I press on through a landscape of fallen boulders and stone 'stacks', one particularly impressive column like a giant sundial, its shadow ticking around the wall of the quarry in which it stands. Sue calls. She's in London. Down the phone I can hear the rumble and groan of traffic and Routemaster buses grinding along Euston Road, the noise of the capital, which in audio terms is not too dissimilar to the sound of a wave crashing on the Cornish shore in my other ear. Maybe she's not outside the British Library at all but waiting for me round the next headland, though my hopes aren't high and are dashed entirely when I hear the voice of a *Big Issue* vendor and the sound of drum 'n' bass pulsing from a car stereo.

Ray and Frankie came to Cornwall to escape the city. They were at the reading last night and told me to call in for a coffee. 'We're right on the path, you can't miss us.' No. 2 The Studio is indeed right on the path, as is a piece of paper with my name written on it pinned to the house sign. I've

just walked down into the valley settlement of Trebarwith
Strand, a community of bungalows and holiday cottages at
the bottom of a cul-de-sac. There's also a gift shop-cum-
mini-market, where I buy a sachet of sun cream and packet
of chewing gum from a man with a pink beard, a pink
moustache, two ear retainers and a head as bald and brown
as a hen's egg. Ray is in the garden, which is a veritable grotto festooned with beach salvage and maritime trophies.
There's a slab on the ground with an e. e. cummings poem
carved into it, near a rough earth wall separating his front
lawn from the Coast Path, under which he's dug a tunnel so
he can access another part of his land without leaving his
property. When I ask him if the powers-that-be are happy
about him excavating a private subway under a National
Trail he shrugs his shoulders, hinting at a long-running saga
and the problems associated with having tens of thousands
of people a year wandering past his gate, not all of them

respectful of boundaries or personal privacy. As if to prove the point a man and a woman coming down the track carrying large rucksacks lean over the wall and begin demanding immediate answers.

'How do I get in?' the woman asks.

'In where?' asks Ray.

'In there, where you are?'

'Why do you want to come in here?'

'For a pot of tea.'

'It isn't a cafe.'

'What?'

'It's not a cafe. It's a house.'

Unsatisfied with the response she says, 'Oh, forget it then,' and they go huffing down the slope in search of refreshment. Ray rolls his eyes. To be fair to the thirsty ramblers the house does have many of the trappings of a beachside cafe and Frankie has just appeared on the patio with hot drinks and a plate of cakes. But to be fair to Ray, if the words 'please' or 'thank you' had been tendered at some point in the conversation he would probably have offered them a cuppa. He leans back on the wooden bench, and Frankie comes and sits on his knee, both of them bronzed of skin and bleached of hair from their thirty-five years in the lap of the cove, in the glare of the sea, under the hob of the sun. Ray wears canvas shoes and no socks. With his foot he points to the massive rock in the middle of the bay, a steep-sided, hump-back loaf of an island, tinged green with weeds and lichen on its upper parts but ringed brown and black where the tide has left its mark. Like almost every other such marooned outcrop in the middle of other such bays along the coast it goes by the name of Gull Rock. Ray says that on two occasions in his life he's swum out and climbed to the top to rebuild the cairn at the summit which is just about visible from here, like a beehive at the very crown of its silhouette. He tells me this with a tone of contented resignation, with the voice and repose of a man who has scaled Gull Rock for the last time perhaps, as if the task of keeping the cairn intact must now fall to a younger member of the tribe. 'It's not easy, mind. You have to pick your way up the fissures to the right, and the whole thing is slimy and stinky with guano. It's really an arête, and even sheerer on the other side, and the gulls don't like to be disturbed. They get very territorial.'

The path out of Trebarwith Strand is blocked with a St Austell's brewery lorry delivering to the Port William Inn on the side of the hill. Once I've made the necessary deviation the ascent takes the form of a series of steps up the side of the valley mouth, steps so steep it's more like climbing a ladder. I count two hundred of them and I'm still not at the top, so sit down to wave to Ray and Frankie in their Aladdin's Cave of buoys, nets, floats and shells before drawing breath and going over the top.

When I'd asked Ray about the walk to Port Isaac he described it as 'hard work'. He didn't know exactly how many combes there were between here and there but seemed to remember there were 'too many, followed by another three'. I've only just about regained consciousness when the first descent opens up at my feet, a near-vertical drop into Backways Cove, and a near-vertical climb up the far side. One thing that has puzzled me on this walk and puzzles me again now is the way in which some valleys have become popular and populated and other seemingly identical valleys are virtually ignored or overlooked. True, there is no road into Backways Cove, but no obvious reason why someone shouldn't or couldn't have built one, and geographically it has very little to distinguish it from Trebarwith Strand. Yet Trebarwith has residents, visitors, a jetty, public toilets, cars, a car park, an inn, a surf shack and a shopkeeper with luminescent facial hair, and Backways Cove has one herring gull peering into a rock pool. I've also been surprised by the relative lack of seabirds all along this walk. The wrong season, maybe, or too much staring at the path and not enough scanning of the skies on my part. Or perhaps I was expecting every stretch of the shoreline to be like Bempton Cliffs, the RSPB reserve on the Yorkshire coast. We were taken there often as kids, and the noise as we walked along the track from the visitors' centre would grow from a distant, low-level crackle, like electrical interference or static, to a full-blown cacophony of squawks and cries once we'd crawled on all fours and peered over the edge. The cliff face itself was a living, writhing wall of birds: gannets, razorbills, puffins and all kinds of gulls perched on hairline cracks in the stone, and the view beyond was a frantic mobile of bodies, beaks and wings, a blizzard of thousands of flying creatures criss-crossing the airspace, some wheeling and soaring, some launching off or coming in to land at breakneck speed, some flapping crazily and comically, others riding the thermals with effortless grace, a swirling mass of birdlife touring the thermal contours, with the occasional shooting star of a gannet spearing diagonally into the waves then clambering back out. Today that solitary gull pecks at its own reflection a couple of times before flapping away to the east. Then a falcon glides over the mouth of the bay and steers inland, halting and hanging on its perch of nothingness, fishing the valley with its eyes.

*

At last night's reading I talked for a while to a woman who was very interested in the effect of landscape on the human psyche, or more particularly the view and its impact on mood. She complained about the number of people she'd observed on the Coast Path, men usually, who seem to have no appreciation whatsoever of the scenery and experience very little of it, who approach the walk as a task and measure their achievement in terms of miles covered, time taken and kilograms carried. And while I agreed with every word she said, I have to acknowledge that on a day like today I'm not far from being one of those men. The unremitting peaks and troughs have started to bring out something very basic in me. They are obstacles to be overcome, problems to be solved, and until I've put them behind me there will be no poetic contemplation of the relationship between topography and spirit, just some head-down walking across hard miles. Hence the route march along Treligga Cliffs, and the route march along Tregardock Cliff, both of them spectacular no doubt to anyone with the time, energy and inclination to notice. And hence my determined indifference towards Jacket's Point and Delabole Point and Ranie Point, and my grumbling descent of the three unnamed ravines which separate them, and the spitting, swearing, sweating effort of clambering back out of them without pausing for thought or photograph, only for gulps of air. For now, facts and figures are my only concerns. I have four miles to go. It is 2.35

p.m. The animal in the field is a cow. There are not three valleys too many as Ray had promised but four. In fact there are five. Make that six. Both my boots are broken. There are three miles to go . . . And so on, and so on. Tiredness is the root cause of this mental fugue but I could also blame it on travelling within an 'inset', a framed and disconnected section of OS Explorer Map Sheet 111 that sits outside the normal space–time continuum in a kind of projected island-otherness several miles off the coast and seemingly in mid-air. I need to reconnect with the mainland, I think. Touch base.

Not until Port Gaverne swings into view do I ease back on the throttle and ease off with the grumpiness, even if it's only to make a note that a cormorant opening its wings on a distant rock forms a fascistic insignia. I also record my first experience of Cornish nationalism in the form of a wooden post with the words 'Kernow – Fuck Off English' scratched aggressively but with a childish hand into the grain. Whoever wants to keep the English out of Cornwall it isn't the Calligraphy and Lettering Arts Society or the Society of Scribes and Illuminators, that's for sure. Hundreds of iridescent and nacreous soap globes, like transparent pearls, are drifting across the road, produced by a mechanically operated bubble-making device in the garden of a house decorated for a child's birthday party. Another sign of civilisation is the now familiar vignette of a chef smoking a cigarette at the kitchen door of a restaurant or pub. Port Isaac, once I've followed the road down into the heart of the town, feels like a bottleneck of people and cars all getting in each other's way, all wanting to be somewhere else at the same time. The pub I'm heading for is at the very bottom of the hill, but to sit in a pub for an hour I need a newspaper, and newspapers are sold at the Co-Op, which is back at the top of the hill. When Tom collects me later in the afternoon and asks me what sort of day I've had, 'Up and down' is the best I can manage.

*

I'm reading at The Poly at Falmouth. On the south coast, where it's warmer, less windy, and the water tastes different. We pass a palm tree in someone's garden and there are big ships in the harbour, proper ones made out of metal. I read here twenty years ago, drove three hundred and fifty miles to speak to an audience of about twenty, then drove three hundred and fifty miles back home that night. There are thirty-eight audience members in the building this evening, some of them undoubtedly the same people as before and probably sitting in the same seats. The mic doesn't work. Every time I twist it back into position it begins to exhibit erectile dysfunction disorder until eventually I push it to one side and decide to shout instead. There's a film being shown in the cinema next door, something with loud guns and vibrating explosions in it. Afterwards, a woman who specialises in giving hugs to travellers gives me a big hug, and a man who has spent time on Tresco tells me that it *is* possible to walk to Bryher and also to Samson, but not to both on the same day. And that the solitary person reported to live there is a ghost. And that I should expect to be sick on the ferry from Penzance to St Mary's. He says, 'They count people on, and they count souls off.' We walk back to Tom's past many galleries on the main street.

They're all closed but low-wattage security lights inside lend the paintings an added dimension of artistry and value. There's an England World Cup qualifier on the TV which has finished by the time we get in. It's a lovely old house. I'm in the back bedroom. I have my own sink. Among the non-monetary items in the sock is a solid, sharp-cornered rectangular object, like a big bar of cooking chocolate swallowed by a snake. Regurgitated it's a book, Heaney's *Human Chain*, a signed copy. I start to read but don't get beyond the first page. The first poem. The first line. 'Had I not been awake.'

Port Isaac to Padstow

Wednesday 11 September

Having slept on the matter, I've come to the conclusion that while the occasional day on my own is necessary and useful, two days walking alone is boring and depressing, and if I don't get some company soon this walk is going to turn into a gloomy, eventless trudge and turn me into a morose, unperceptive robo-hiker. Somehow, the more I'm distracted, the more I notice. So it's with relief and a welcoming tone that I say hello to complete strangers Michael, Jane and Millie at the rendezvous point near the public toilets at the top of Port Isaac, and with surprise then admiration that I watch them organise an impromptu bar on the car-park wall, Jane mixing the vodka and tomato juice that make up the Bloody Mary, Michael adding the seasoning and spices, and Millie inserting enormous sticks of celery as the finishing touch. Having sworn a vow of temperance until the walk is done I opt for the virgin version of the same cocktail, but still feel a little vicarious rush of giddiness as the real drinkers knock back the lurid red potion and the Smirnoff kicks into their circulation and their conversation, bringing colour to their faces and vocabularies. Once they're fuelled up we drop down into the deserted town and climb the narrow road, which becomes a path on the far side, ignoring Fern Cottage, home to the fictional Doc Martin from the TV series of the same name, which I've never watched but am happy to believe is cosy Sunday-night eyewash. Jane is the sister of singer-songwriter Tom McRae; I wrote the sleeve notes for one of his albums and once penned a song lyric for him called 'Nurofen Breakfast'. Michael doesn't formally introduce himself but over the next three or four miles, via overheard comments and a bit of surreptitious Googling on my phone, I deduce that he is very probably a comedy writer and co-creator of *Who Wants to Be a Million-aire?*. He's carrying a Tupperware box of Earl Grey cupcakes, which he thinks he might work up into a proposal for a new Channel 4 walking programme, *Around Britain with a Box of Cupcakes*. 'I've seen worse shows,' he says. 'You've written some of them,' adds Millie, his daughter, a budding playwright with such a passion for language that she's tattooed a favourite line from a Ted Hughes poem onto her ankle. 'Did you clear copyright permission?' I ask her. She didn't, she replies, and neither did she get agreement from the F. Scott Fitzgerald estate to have a sentence from *The Great Gatsby* inked into her flesh, though she's less forthcoming about the physical whereabouts of that quote. I take a slug of south Cornish water from a bottle filled from Tom's kitchen tap in Falmouth this morning. For health reasons, Millie wasn't sure she'd make it more than a few hundred yards up the first hill, but either the vodka or the cupcakes or both have provided enough impetus to get her all the way to the tiny inlet of Port Quin. At my request she sits down on the harbour wall, unlaces her floral-patterned air-cushioned leather boot, and there between the top of her pink sock and the bottom of her black leggings, written in grey-green italics, are the words, 'What happens in the heart simply happens.' I'm not aware that anyone has ever etched a line of my own poetry indelibly into their skin, though after a reading I once signed someone's forehead with a biro. At his request, I should add. He was a strange-looking lad with big glasses and a broken nose, and stranger still with my moniker scrawled across his brow. He said, 'Cheers, man. I'm gonna get it framed.'

Then it's just me again, ploughing on. The dry rubbery shrubs that line the path are mallow, and the plant that casts its green and pink webbing over the gorse is dodder. Twenty-two black-headed gulls have alighted on the inlet below me and are all lined up in the same direction, like a weather omen, but presaging what? At the top of the hill there's Doyden Castle, more like a small chapel with a round window in the design of the VW logo, or so it looks from the distance at which I pass, after which I wander around the

lip of a gaping hole in the earth, a disused mineshaft or collapsed sea cave with a partially fenced circumference, and I
kick a few rabbit droppings into the gaping orifice. In the
next valley, three people are clearing gorse from a section of
the path, a man and a woman with savage-looking petrol-
driven brush-cutters swinging from sturdy harnesses, carv-
ing away at the woody trunks and roots, and to peer into the
twisted and knotted undergrowth is to witness a shadowy
understorey rendered lifeless and lightless by that dense,
greedy, all-consuming shrub. The air is perfumed with the
coconut of the flowers, the menthol of the spiky needles, the
smell of sawn timber and the slight tinge of smoke where
the blades have scorched and smouldered against the harder, thicker stems. A third man, who might be a volunteer or
could be repaying a debt to society in the form of community service, has been given the less glamorous task of collecting the felled branches by hand and throwing them onto
teetering piles at the side of the track.

I heard an interview on the radio this morning with a
man who is currently swimming from John O'Groats to
Land's End, who must be travelling parallel to me at the
moment and whose physical and psychological endeavours
make my own trip look like a walk in the park. I'd mentioned him to Jane, and we'd talked about long solo journeys and their effects on the body and brain. She'd told me
about the microlight pilot Brian Milton, who she knows,
and how on his flight from London to Sydney he became
convinced that someone was with him in the one-man flying machine, a sensation that he was not alone. And we
talked about a man who had recently canoed around the
outline of the British Isles on his own, who described pad-

dling into a remote, inaccessible bay on the west coast of Scotland and having the distinct feeling that no human had ever set foot on its beach before. There's no such sense of discovery or of entering uncharted territory along this well-worn path, and yet the land is new to me, with each stretch of coastline unfurling and unfolding in unexpected directions and dimensions, so ideas of anticipation and exploration are never too far away. And even though I haven't reached the stage where I feel the presence of a mysterious spectral person walking alongside, after so many miles of hiking and so many days away from home it's disarming to realise that a great many of the conversations I've had along the way have not been with walking companions or the organisers of my readings or the providers of my beds and breakfasts or the conveyors of the Galapagos Tortoise, but with myself. And one or two arguments as well.

*

For the time being the path has levelled out, cruising at a low and steady altitude, and the view ahead is dominated by the Pentire Headland, which juts out Sphinx-like into the sea. Taking the opportunity to file a damage report I note an aching sensation in my groin, a straining sensation in my left thigh and an intermittent but sharp pain at the base of my second toe on my right foot which is particularly acute when walking uphill. But the biggest problem is my boots, which are falling apart at an alarming daily rate and which are beginning to look like the boots of a tramp. They wouldn't be out of place on the feet of Vladimir or Estragon. I'll keep going in them on the basis that I don't really have an alternative for the time being, no team of pit mechanics standing by and no second set of tyres, but will have to figure out a Plan B in the longer term, especially if the weather turns. There's a big Cornish flag flapping on a set of rocks called The Mouls, and I diligently circumnavigate the whole headland even though there's a much-used short-cut across the neck, then sit down on a bench, among a miniature graveyard of wooden crosses and paper poppies, next to the memorial stone inscribed with Laurence Binyon's famous poem elegising soldiers lost in the First World War. Situated on the brink of an overhanging promontory, the uninitiated could be forgiven for thinking that the words 'FOR THE FALLEN' commemorate visitors to these cliffs who strayed too close to the edge. Lunch is a doorstep of brown bread and Cornish Yarg, including its nettle-leaf rind. In Polzeath, the smart and trendy resort hiding in the nick of the next bend, someone forgot to mention the current economic recession and the stagnation of the building industry, because roofers are tiling, scaffolders are erecting, and the narrow streets to the north side of the bay are busy with mini diggers, cement mixers and deliveries of timber and stone. On the south side a pair of lifeguards in their beachside hut are visible only by the two sets of suntanned feet resting on the windowsill next to two mugs of steaming tea, and in the car park behind I watch a woman pushing her knee into the small of her husband's back as she tries to zip up his very tight wetsuit, shouting at him to 'breathe in, Roger. BREATHE IN.' The sandy bay in between is full of surfers, dozens of vertical black marks against the yellow background, with dozens of smaller black blobs bobbing around in the waves. Like a Lowry painting but without the clogs. Fancy white wooden houses line the flat grassy strip towards Daymer Bay, where I cut inland and head down a leafy, thirties-style lane that could be an illustration from Betjeman's *Shell Guide to Cornwall*, an entirely appropriate approach given that it leads eventually to the resting place of the former Poet Laureate himself. First, though, the visiting literary pilgrim must run the gauntlet of two fairways, keeping to a strictly enforced footpath across the sandy links of St Enodoc Golf Club, and I risk battery by golf ball and/or bollocking by golfer when I stop to watch a foursome of retirees hitting what appear to be casual or tired tee shots that roll and roll to within about six feet of the pin. According to some sources, for over three hundred years St Enodoc's Church lay partly buried in sand, and to maintain its status as a consecrated place of worship parishioners would dig down through the roof of the building twice a year to hold Christian services. Fully excavated and restored in the nineteenth century it still has a submerged appearance, with only the twisted witch's hat of the spire visible above a high tamarisk hedge. A set of steps lead down through the lychgate into the enclosed graveyard and Betjeman's grave is immediately on the right, his name and dates carved in flowery letters among curly patterns on a thin, round-headed sheet of slate, with a pot of pink azaleas growing beneath it. Inside the church a motion-activated light comes on when visitors walk up the aisle to inspect the kneelers stitched with birds, plants and woodland creatures. From the honesty stall I buy a couple of postcards and a biro that doesn't work. Outside, three golfers in Rupert Bear outfits and peeling single calf-skin gloves from their hands have just entered the churchyard, their metal spikes grinding on the stone path. With his unsheathed finger one of them points to Sir John's resting place, saying, 'There he is. What's-his-face.' On the nearby green the three tripods of their bags are propped up on spindly legs, like over-sized insects, next to three little white eggs.

I leave the path after Brea Hill and walk along the shore-line to catch the ferry across the estuary from Rock, then follow other disembarked passengers into the bottleneck of Padstow, which is rammed with more people than I've seen since Butlins. On the near side of the harbour I lean on the railings, star-struck by a Frank Sinatra impersonator croon-ing his way through several Sinatra classics. He's got all the clothes, all the moves, a captive audience galleried on the steps above him and by my calculations about fifty quid an hour raining into the battered, brown leather suitcase lying open-jawed on the pavement. Never mind walking ump-teen miles a day and reading umpteen poems at night, here is an object lesson in busking. Stand next to an ice-cream van, press 'play' on the stereo, click your fingers every once in a while and let the crowd come to you. A different crowd every hour of the day, every day of the week, the whole summer long. He's hitting all the right notes, and I take my hat off to him.

*

Merryn intercepts me in the bus-station car park just when I was contemplating upping my calorific intake with some posh fish and chips from Rick Stein's takeaway across the road. There isn't even room in the boot of her tiny car for a rucksack, let alone my stick, which relative to the vehicle

ACK OF RIBS, ¼ ROAST CHICKEN, MIXE)
S, GRILLED GAMMON STEAK, RUMP S
AK, FILLET STEAK, RIBEYE STEAK,
AK, BEEF & ALE CASSEROLE, FISHERMAN
KKA MASALA, ROASTED VEGETABLE CHEESE
RED THAI CURRY, CHUNKY CHILLI CON CAR
ETABLE CURRY, VEGETABLE QUICHE,
RRAINE, COTTAGE PIE, LASAGNE VERDI
LASAGNE, CLIPPER LUNCH, GRILLED
S LUNCH, PLOUGHMAN'S LUNCH, HALIBU
LUNCH, JOHN DORY FILLETS, SALMON S
INIERE, GRILLED SEABASS, RAINBOW TRO
MON SOLE, GRILLED PLAICE, OCEAN PL
ALAD, SEAFOOD AU GRATIN, TUNA SALA
RESSED CRAB WHOLE LOBSTER COOKED IN
BSTER SALAD, CORNISH WHITE CRAB MEAT S

suddenly looks like a caber or telegraph pole and has to be ingeniously manoeuvred into the back, where I sit with my bag slung papoose-style over my chest and my knees up by my ears. Merryn drives, and is given instructions and directions from the passenger seat by her co-pilot Kerris, her colleague from the library. I can't begin to imagine how bad I must smell. Even to myself I smell bad, so the pong must be truly nauseating to two smartly dressed librarians in such cramped confinement. Merryn opens a window, politely stating 'condensation' as the reason, and Kerris dutifully leans towards the console and turns the blower up to full. We drive to a residential area on the hillside above Wadebridge, where I perform a minor feat of escapology to exit the car and leave my stinking, broken boots on the step, looking for somewhere to hitch them for the night before entering the house. The voice shouting, 'Here wends the weary traveller,' from the downstairs kitchen belongs to Merryn's husband Mike, who is standing with a bottle of something half decent in his hand and whose face drops slightly when I tell him I'm on the wagon. We say grace before eating, and two stray chickens peck at the French windows, begging for scraps. Kerris is still here, sitting down to the meal and helping herself to tea and biscuits, then heading off upstairs announcing that she is going to take a shower. The weather forecast for tomorrow is poor. In fact it's already raining, just a quiet, damping wetness but enough to put paid to Mike's suggestion that I could sit in the garden and write. Instead he settles me in an armchair in the front room under an anglepoise lamp next to a cup of tea, and closes the kitchen door to prevent the sounds of washing-up and other domestic chores disturbing the hushed reverence a poet needs to compose his mind and his verse, and I fall asleep.

*

The modern bungalow-style Wadebridge Library stands next to the old railway station with its solid Cornish stonework and wooden canopy, part of which now houses the

John Betjeman Centre. For his sense of rhythm and rhyme, his eye for the changing twentieth century, his pin-sharp social observations and his playful sarcasm, Betjeman found admirers and secured his pages in the grand anthologies of British poetry. But to those who see no further than his cuddly 'teddy bear' image or are turned off by the air of public-school Victorian Englishness that informed his views, characterised his television persona and infused his voice, a disused railway station on a disused branch line in a small country town would seem his perfect terminus. The library is closed on Wednesdays but Merryn and her team have opened the doors, rolled back the stacks and arranged the seating around my reading position in front of the Pets and Garden Design sections. With Merryn, colleague Kerris, myself and five modestly proportioned paperback books in the car there isn't room for Mike, so he has jogged all the way, possibly across several lawns or newly mown playing fields because he arrives with wet grass cuttings stuck to his shoes and the bottom of his trouser legs. The Bloody Mary team from this morning turn up, and as a cautionary tale for Millie I read 'The Clown Punk', about a man with a heavily tattooed face. Every town has one. And I wonder out loud what happened to the boy in the care home where I used to work who had inked the words 'Halifax Town AFC' into the back of his hands and forearms. That was in the late eighties, before the team began slipping away into relegation and administration. At twelve years old he was already nursing a sense of rejection from his family. What is he like at forty, with his skin and limbs insolubly dedicated to another failed allegiance, another lost cause, to an officially *dissolved* club? After the reading a woman from my home village of

Marsden comes over to talk to me, wondering if I remember her brother, who was my age and in my class at school. I tell her that I remember him very well because on one occasion he drew a goldfinch in my jotter, which I can still picture in my mind's eye, on the left-hand page of the lined notepad, with its red face inside a white collar and black hood, and the crayoned yellow bars of its wings. Later that day my parents were waiting for me in the car on the road above the playground. I opened the book and showed them the bird, in all its magnificent detail, in all its colourful glory.

'Who drew that?' my mum asked.

'I did,' I said.

'No, you didn't,' said my dad.

'Yes, I did.'

'No, you didn't.'

'Yes, I did.'

'No, you didn't.'

'Yes, I did.'

I didn't, but it hurt that he wouldn't believe my lie. That evening he came into my room to say goodnight. 'I did draw that bird,' I told him. He grinned and pulled the cord that turned out the light. 'OK, you did,' he said. Then as he was closing the door added, 'But you didn't.'

The woman from Marsden says, 'Thank you for remembering my brother.'

'How is he?'

She says, 'When he was little he used to make carousels out of paper and cardboard. Little fairground rides.' Behind her glasses her eyes have become tearful. The chairs have been stacked in piles and someone is waiting to lock up and set the alarm.

*

Back at Merryn and Mike's I'm sleeping in the study, on the sofa bed, under the all-seeing eye of a wide-screen Apple Mac. Kerris has come back with us, and from the framed photographs dotted around the house of a girl with a similar face at various stages of childhood I have finally figured out that she is their daughter. My companions in the room are two Garfields, one sitting on the mantelpiece and one leaning nonchalantly against a vase, plus two small teddies and a crucified Christ.

Padstow to Constantine Bay

9.5 MILES

Thursday 12 September

The smoke alarm wakes me up. Mike is cooking breakfast and the alarm goes off when the bacon is ready. Kerris is making free with the toast and condiments, as she is perfectly entitled to as a member of the family. As I am the only person capable of lifting it, Merryn suggests I put the Galapagos Tortoise in the car ready for the handover later in the day, then I slide in next to it, half expecting the vehicle to tip backwards and the bonnet to rise into the air.

This morning Padstow is unrecognisable from the place that elbowed and jostled me yesterday afternoon. We've walked down through the graveyard of St Petroc's, Mike and myself, 'God's acre' with its sculpted yews and the lavish candelabra of a large magnolia tree. A couple of delivery wagons are unloading on the main street but other than that it's a ghost town, the first ferry from Rock arriving with no one on it. In fact the only visitor at this hour is the tide, which has completely covered the sandy beaches on both sides of the estuary and is nudging and bumping insistently at the pier wall. A small sailing boat called *Timbobbin* heads tentatively out of the harbour when the hydraulic barrier is raised, and mid-channel a dredger is scooping up great jawfuls of the Doom Bar, the underwater sandbank at the mouth of the Camel on which hundreds of boats have foundered, which has given its name to a local beer (on which, no doubt, many

[181]

have likewise foundered) and which was formed as a result of a mermaid's curse. Huge cabbage fields sweep down to the path all the way from Gun Point to the mini jungle in the valley behind Harbour Cove, where the sand lies golden and undisturbed and which Mike describes as a 'local beach', meaning without facilities and not accessible by vehicle. The small settlement of Hawker's Cove is emblazoned with 'PRIVATE' notices at every turn and gateway, and the path obeys, kowtowing and curtseying between the covered boats and the renovated coastguard cottages, slaloming and limbo-ing around awkwardly parked, uncompromisingly large estate cars. Passing the last house a dog barks from the other side of a high-panelled fence and a hutch full of guinea pigs witter and squeal like short-wave radio or dial-up internet. Mike is a walking, talking map of local geography and a textbook of marine science, and as Dr Michael Kent, author of *Cornwall from the Coast Path*, the perfect guide and companion for this leg of the journey. He tells me about his PhD on the life cycle of the spiny cockle, which he conducted in Torbay but abandoned after only finding three of them. And about sitting and watching evening primroses open their papery, pale-yellow flowers at the back end of the day on the coastline around here. And about how the black cliff faces, such as those near Boscastle, are actually covered in tar lichen, a rich, dense, living entity which colonises the stone and is a sign of life and health. And how he walked around Pentire Point every day for a year, including Christmas Day, his birthday and the birthdays of his family, compiling a three-hundred-and-sixty-five-day photographic record and written logbook of the headland. And how he once hiked around the whole of Cornwall in sixteen days, camping rough every night and taking just two lots of clothes with him: a dry set to sleep in and another set which he climbed back into every morning, no matter how wet. He tells me that the brown, sure-footed, goat-like sheep on the cliff slopes are Soay, and that the docile cattle are mostly Devon Reds. But his true field of interest and expertise is the humble limpet. How they 'farm' particular areas and get territorial with other limpets that stray into the wrong patch, sometimes bulldozing their competitors right off the face of the rock. On quiet evenings with the tide out, the background noise is the sound of thousands of active limpets rasping and grinding away. A group of squaddies on a training exercise once ridiculed him when he told them limpets were a fantastic source of free protein for people out in the wild. To prove it he popped a raw one in his mouth and chewed on the salty, slimy, rubbery pellet, and didn't grimace or retch until they were out of sight. I do the same thing with a strand of samphire he picks from the cleft in a herringbone wall and offers to me as a mid-morning snack. We pass the daymark tower, a non-illuminating lighthouse erected for navigational purposes, and circumnavigate a big round hole in the earth, a collapsed sea cave in the middle of a ploughed field. An elderly couple approach it from the other direction, peer down into the abyss for a few seconds then walk away, as if it's a ritual they've been practising every day of their lives. We picnic above Harlyn Bay, looking out to the tubular blue lifeboat station with its stilts and runway, like something that might launch a nuclear warhead rather than a rescue boat, under the large caravan ghetto at Mother Ivey's Bay. We had fancied a bench a mile or so further back but it was occupied by a sleeping elderly man with

Padstow . . .

his suitcase at his side and what appeared to be all his worldly goods in various holdalls and carrier bags, just after a gate with the words 'I Hate Snobs. Posh Scum' written in marker pen across the top bar. The mist has come down, thick and silver, so we're rounding Trevose Head before I've realised that we're on it, and when the lighthouse suddenly materialises above me, a white, spectral form in the ashen fog, present yet invisible at the same time, looming and horribly near, I duck for cover. The scrubby quarry on the other side of the service road is the kind of place where Dr Who's TARDIS would have landed in the Tom Baker era. At Booby's Bay, lifeguard personnel and equipment outnumber all other forms of human life and activity by an infinitive proportion, there being no one and nothing on the beach that isn't red and yellow or blonde and tanned, though there may be surfers and swimmers out beyond the curtain of fog, which has reduced visibility to about a quarter of a mile. We're nearly at our destination and in plenty of time, so it's OK to stop for ten minutes to inspect the abundance of creamy white flowers growing around a brick cottage at the edge of Trevose Golf Club, floppy cream petals cupping showy yellow stamens, virginal and sexualised at the same time, both staid and erotic, which Mike thinks might be burnet rose.

*

Treyarnon YHA is full of bedraggled tourists sheltering from the poor weather, waiting for cheese paninis and trying to connect to the wi-fi network. Merryn arrives in her toy car, and I ransom Mike for my luggage then wait for Stuart, the next link in the chain, who is described in my notes as a brewer but arrives in a red van rather than on a dray pulled by shire horses. The Galapagos Tortoise slides into the back next to a pile of tubes and pumps and we set off into the interior. To arrive at a white-painted farmhouse in a small hamlet on the brow of a hill, where we're skittled by a young black puppy hurtling and skidding around a tiled kitchen floor, testing every material element of the world with its pointed teeth. I sit in the window seat in my allocated bedroom for half an hour, collecting thoughts, making notes, watching blue tit, great tit, coal tit, chaffinch, siskin, greenfinch, yellowhammer, sparrow and nuthatch making raids on the bird-feeder in front of a badminton net which droops and drips across the lawn, weighed down by moisture in the air, harvesting the fog, distilling the rain. A pair of collared doves watch unblinkingly and motionless from the pergola.

As a stranger in a strange house, and without embarking on some kind of Sherlockian interpretation of evidence and clues, I usually try to fix on an object that speaks about the people who live here and their implied values, or radiates a particular vibe. It helps generate conversation, it satisfies a certain amount of curiosity, and more importantly it can help to steer me away from saying the wrong thing. It's not that I want to play the part of a sycophantic social chameleon or political quick-change artist charming his way from one family to the next, but on a journey that has relied on hospitality and generosity from lefty white-collar workers, entrepreneurial business owners, liberal artisans, expert scientists, practising Christians, regional managers and high-ranking aristocrats, I've found it easier to listen first and talk later. So the pile of *Resurgence & Ecologist* magazines next to the loo, for example, I take as a signal of attitude and lifestyle in the Thomson household, and the theme is continued as Stuart tours me around the farmstead, joined by daughters Amber and Willow, who skip and swing through an autumnal plantation of hazel, alder, sweet chestnut and yew. We're followed by a pair of comical Indian runner ducks with their stretched necks, prim upright stance and busybody waddle, like well-to-do gossips at a church fete. The garden path curls through patches of raspberry, gooseberry, greengage, past olive and fig trees, through glasshouses and polytunnels of incubating tomato, cucumber, ginger and gherkin, and past trees dripping with elderberries and stooping with apples and plums. In the middle of this Garden of Eden, and the thing that we actually stepped outside to see, is a solar panel that tilts and rotates as it tracks the daily arc of the sun, a piece of equipment so large and serious that standing at the side of it for a photograph Stuart looks like a schoolboy on a

day trip to Jodrell Bank. He's actually something of a computer software wizard, but when he's not coding and programming he's chief cook and bottle-washer, literally, of the Atlantic Brewery, producing hand-made, bottle-conditioned, organic ales in little more than a converted garage behind the house. The kids have gone off to round up the chickens, and in the kitchen I meet Sarah, who is doing her PhD on the politics of school playground design, many of which are being designed by the same companies who build prisons, apparently. I watch her crumbling meringue nests into a bowl of strawberries and cream for another heart-clogging Cornish dessert, and Stuart is now chopping crudités and running a slicing wheel across the LP-sized veggie pizzas, ready for the guests. It's a back-handed compliment, but for the first time on this journey I feel comfortable and relaxed enough to ask the folks I'm staying with if I can put my underwear in their washing machine.

*

Because their eighteenth-century house wasn't especially designed for recitation or performance, the reading is a split-screen event, with the audience of family and friends seated either side of a partition wall and me in the middle, broadcasting sometimes to the dining room on the right and sometimes to the living room on the left. Stuart has 'tapped' a cask of Atlantic Pilgrim in my honour, and because it would be churlish and ungrateful to refuse I sip from a pint of the honey-coloured beer between poems. Later in the evening he shows me into a room at the back where a pub-style beer pump is clamped to the edge of a worktop and connected to a barrel, from which I can help myself. After a couple of weeks without a drink, even a modest intake of alcohol has an immediate and powerful effect, clouding my thoughts, melting my tongue, dissolving my limbs. Not so much nectar, more like morphine, entering my bloodstream, flowing through my veins and stirring my dreams.

Constantine Bay to Newquay

13 MILES

Friday 13 September

Neptune might live here. This could be Poseidon's house. Ivy climbs along a fence made of sea-weathered planks and timbers that look like they've come from sunken galleons or ships of the line. Dozens of round plastic floats like faded royal orbs from distant kingdoms are situated here and there, some strung on lengths of nylon rope or hanging like baubles from branches and hooks, some nestled in corners like the eggs of fabulous birds, others sitting in the grass like luminous turnips or severed heads. A big white lifebelt like a toilet seat is hoopla-ed over an upright post. Three rickety deckchairs are positioned on the roof of a makeshift shelter. Alongside brooms and spades the bones of large sea creatures lean against an outside wall.

Playwright, actor, poet, lobster fisherman, campaigner, politician and filmmaker Nick Darke spent years collecting what the sea had deposited in the long-by-narrow inlet of Porthcothan Beach, partly as an exercise in de-littering the shoreline in front of his house, partly as a method of accumulating free-of-charge material resources, but increasingly as a way of monitoring the sea's moods and movements and the activities of those who use it, even from as far away as four thousand miles. What I would call beachcombing he called wrecking, and what I would call salvage he called wreck. By following up the serial numbers and company names on

buoys, floats and all kinds of flotsam and jetsam, he not only tracked down the manufacturers and owners of much of the equipment but opened up a dialogue with fishermen and trawlermen on the other side of the Atlantic, whose lost property and discarded trammel washed up at his front door. Nick Darke died in 2005 but his widow, the filmmaker, writer, painter and poet Jane Darke, still goes wrecking along the coast and recording what the ocean has delivered into her lap, and keeps adding wreck to the house, to the point where it's difficult to see where the original structure ends and where adornment and ornament begins. Inside it's no different, every room I peer into being a museum, storehouse or gallery of found objects. Photographs, notebooks, artefacts and drawings from artistic projects, works in progress and abandoned ideas occupy every available surface. Jane ushers Stuart and myself towards the dining room for what is our second cooked meal in the space of two hours, a delicious and

unusual psychosexual combination of black pudding and
figs, the figs plucked from a tree whose lower branches want
to deliver their fruit right to the table by reaching in through
the window. With every ingredient and course being served
on beautifully uncoordinated antique crockery and ornate
silverware it feels less like a full English and more like a
Roman banquet or a ceremonial feast. And there's something
opulent and spiritual about Jane herself, a kind of priestess of
Porthcothan with her arcane knowledge and instinctive
understanding of how the weather and the deep will lay
down their offerings at her feet. It also occurs to me that
what she practises here is more than just a form of recycling,
it's environmental alchemy, finding not only a practical purpose in the lumps of driftwood and the jawbones of whales
but honouring their existence in this world, transforming
waste and junk into art. In fact the whole house is an installation of a kind worthy of the Turner Prize shortlist, though
not nearly self-conscious or self-regarding enough to win.
If my journey is an Odyssey, then Jane is its Circe, turning
Stuart and myself into swine by dishing up a second helping
of fried pig's blood, and to fulfil her mythological role she
must now show us where to go next, putting on her waterproof coat and leading us down through the garden, past the
giant red sphere of a metal buoy with the words 'Falmouth
Massachusetts' written on it and out through the secret door
in the wreck fence.

*

We'd set out just after eight, which now feels several hours
ago, Sarah having handed over a neat pile of socks and

underpants still warm from the tumble drier, their two girls all ironed and combed and ready for school, Stuart letting the beer brew on its own for a day. The weather forecast on the radio is pretty diabolical. Sarah says, 'People come here in the summer holidays, spend a fortnight on the beach and fall in love with the place. They sell up and move to Cornwall. Then it's September. They open their front door and it's like someone's thrown a bucket of water in their face.' Rosie runs us to the starting point at Treyarnon. I don't get the full story but she might be Stuart and Sarah's lodger or tenant, occupying part of the homestead I didn't see last night. What isn't in doubt is her day job as a lifeguard, something I could have guessed at from her yellow hair, long legs, powerful shoulders, beach-bum tan and the ageing hatchback full of sandwich wrappers, fag packets, sand, and with a Sex-Wax air freshener dangling from the rear-view mirror. For many who spend their summer days along the shores of Cornwall, work and play appear inseparable, interchangeable, and to my eyes indistinguishable. It's foggy rather than rainy, and we pass a number of isolated rocks just off the coast, like little cartoon countries with grassed plateaus above vertical black cliffs, though all uninhabited and uninhabitable except to seabirds which are too far away and too vague in the mist to confidently identify. Beyond Jane's house the thick low cloud begins to condense and weep, the wind picks up and the air turns colder, a south-easterly delivering showers then full-on rain as we pick our way carefully along the crumbling cliffs that overlook a succession of high, inaccessible coves. Jane points out a small green buoy in the foaming, roiling water in Boatman's Cove which marks one of her lobster pots, then points to the cross-section of cliff face on the opposing head-

land, all stone apart from the thinnest crust of soil, making fishing the only viable form of harvest for anyone living this close to the sea. Gorse and heather are scrounging what few nutrients the earth can hold onto. 'Good wrecking-light weather,' I say to Jane. But on the whole she's dismissive of stories of avaricious and heartless locals tying lanterns to the tails of donkeys to lure vessels onto the rocks. There's always been enough booty making its way onto the shore, she insists, especially around Porthcothan, which is a natural collection pool for floating and drifting debris, especially after a few days of storm. When I ask about her most intriguing finds she's torn between the big red float in her garden, the many exotic beans and seed pods that have made it all the way from South America, and the number of dildos and blow-up dolls that wash ashore. 'Sailors. At sea.' We talk about local poets, and she jokes that down here you're either Clemo (Jack Clemo, the deeply Cornish and devoutly Christian poet who died in 1994) or Causley (Charles Causley, the deeply Cornish poetic balladeer and tale-teller who died in 2003) but rarely both. Then at a turn in the track she tells us she's heading off to see a friend, over there, pointing into the blur of weather that forms a grey wall at the other side of the sodden heath, and disappears into the mist. Only to be replaced by Richard, an English teacher at the English public school which gave us both the machine-gun scene in the Lindsay Anderson film *if . . .* and serial soft-rockers Keane. He's also something of a surfer, he reveals, which prompts the same confession from Stuart, and I walk on ahead while they trade surfing vocabulary and form a kindred bond via the exchange of privileged information on the subjects of secret beaches and legendary waves. Out in front on a path full of puddles flanked by fog to each side and with the sea nowhere in sight I could be on the Pennine Way, and for a few miles begin to feel almost at home. My boots are not just wet, they are drowned. If I stamp my feet water spurts from the ankle cuffs and geysers erupt from holes in the seams. We make a respectful detour around yet another yawning abyss in the ground, and half an hour later must look a sorry sight as we huddle in the smoking shelter outside a seaside pub in the ghost town of Mawgan Porth, eating our butties among dead cigarettes and the stale odour of spilt beer. Richard goes inside for a pee and comes back out saying, 'You won't believe this but it's heaving in there.' And I don't.

Rounding Stem Point, just as the elongated view of
Watergate Bay opens up before us, Richard spots a dolphin,
then a second, until seven or eight are darning the water,
enough to call a pod, with dozens and dozens of surfers only
yards away but entirely unaware of the dolphins' presence
and their hypnotic, effortless motion through the water.
We're heading towards Newquay, the most populated place
on my journey with just shy of twenty thousand permanent
residents, a Mecca for UK surfers, and more recently a mag-
net for stag and hen parties, especially since the arrival of
low-budget airlines at the airport up the road. It was in a
moment of masochistic bloody-mindedness that I turned
down more reserved offers and chose instead to give a reading in the middle of the town on a Friday night, against what
I assume will be a background of puking grooms, braying
brides and the commingling of their respective entourages
dressed as knights or cowgirls and decorated with inflated

condoms. Putting poetry to the test against the hubbub of holidaymakers in a region defined by tourism was always part of the plan, and considered in those terms there could hardly be a better stage for the contest. But now the day has come I've started to wonder why I didn't just play safe and opt for a church hall in the suburbs or a scout hut in an outlying village. Richard tells me not to worry: he had his stag do here and it was fine, though a quarter of an hour later he's still talking me through some of the 'highlights' and has convinced me that before sunset I'm going to be swept up in a mixed-gender, semi-naked conga and photographed doing 'Oops Up Side Your Head' on a revolving dance floor with some of Jane's more exotic beach finds gaffer-taped to my limbs and smoking a rolled-up copy of my *Selected Poems*.

Geographically speaking Newquay is a complicated place with several bays and beaches and as many clusters of shops and houses, so when we arrive at Porth Beach I'm not sure if we're actually in the town or in yet another place with the word 'Porth' in its name, of which there have been many already and more to come. We're staring down into the deep gulley of the cove because we're looking for sand artist Tony Plant, who has invited me to watch him at work. He makes shapes in the beach and documents his art with a remote-control time-lapse camera, before the tide turns and washes the canvas clean. I suspect he might have been rained off, but through the murk he eventually comes into focus, sheltering in a cave on the other side of the valley with the beginnings or the abandoned remains of a swirly shell-shaped pattern which starts by the rock pools and finishes about halfway down the beach. From up here, by the pitch 'n' putt, he looks like a cute little sea elf in his cavern or grotto, but closer up he's a tall, powerfully built man with a shaved head and a serious expression on his face. He's not just making sandcastles, or sand sculptures of fire-breathing dragons, or sand palaces with tea lights in the windows, usually constructed close to the prom from where appreciative tourists can toss loose change into a plastic cup. He's making art, though what he does is appealing in its simplicity: it's just him, in his bare feet, with a garden rake, taking a walk around a flat wet beach, scoring his abstract designs into the surface of the earth. How he earns a living I've no idea, given that there's no actual product and the effects are temporary and he has no ownership of the land he inscribes or copyright over the lines he incises. I find myself making mental comparisons with my own marks on a blank surface, and wondering how I'd feel if I got up one morning to find the slate wiped clean, the pages bare, the lines erased. Of course, at some level it's all impermanent: everything

will fade away or vanish eventually, it's a question of when, not if, and maybe that's what Tony's sand art is saying. Stop thinking of the everlasting because it doesn't exist. Just be present in the moment, then start over.

'Can I have a go?'

'Sure.'

'What do I do?'

'Hold the rake behind you and walk into space.'

I trundle around the outside of an outswinging curve that Tony had started, turning round now and again to check the rake is clawing its seven or eight furrows parallel with his own, and to the same depth, and follow the outline into a spiral that loops the loop several times before sling-shooting me out along another curling and circling section of the pattern, listening to the whispering of the metal fingers in the wet, gritty sand. It's oddly pleasing, to see a shape emerging and growing, and to be practising a kind of unreadable graf fiti on such a large scale in such a public place without causing any particular damage or offence. It's only when I go 'off piste' that things don't feel right, arcing away from Tony's expansive and flowing design to add my own little flourish, because what unfolds is neither formless nor formed, neither fish nor fowl, just some meaningless childish squiggle out of kilter with the original, out of sympathy with the beach and out of scale with the bay. It's harder than it looks, the lack of restrictions and the limitless possibilities only adding to the difficulty. Like writing free verse – all that empty page to go at and every word in the dictionary to choose from. From the next beach I look back and see Tony still walking into space, a wandering tripod of two long legs and a stiff rake trailing behind, generating his magnified Spirograph in the sand. I'm trying to see if he's found a way of incorporating my own ham-fisted scribblings into his work or is busily effacing them with his practised curlicues and swirls, but his is a cartographic art, only fully appreciated from above, so at this elevation – which is sea level and therefore no elevation at all – I can't say. And once the tide has come and gone I'll never know.

*

The co-owner of Cafe Irie has a contemporary beard, piercings, no aitch in his spelling of Jon and sells pumpkin seeds on the counter of his hippy-shack coffee house. All of which leads me to believe I'm in good hands for the evening. Among the fleshpots and hotspots of Friday-night Newquay this could well be the only venue in town suitable for poetry. The reading is upstairs, away from the gurgle of the cappuccino-maker, among scatter cushions and old settees. It's not a big room but it's cosy and atmospherically lit. I'm reading near the window, and in the diagonally opposite corner a filmmaker called Jo has set up her camera and somehow managed to squeeze behind it to get some wide-angle shots of 'audience reaction' to the poems. Fainting, fitting, speaking in tongues, involuntary weeping, uncontrollable applause, standing ovations – that kind of thing. As well as a film director, camera operator and sound recordist she's also a singer-songwriter with tours under her belt, a backing band behind her and albums to her name (or rather her nom de plume – she goes under the alias of Josie Ghost). The words 'Don't think twice' are tattooed on one of her hands, and 'It's alright' on the other. I do think twice:

about the skin of Porth Beach now washed and reset by the tide, then about the hands of a young woman permanently etched with a Bob Dylan lyric that reads as a mantra in self-motivation as well as a provocative and potentially dangerous open-ended invitation, and about the Clown Punk and the boy with the name of a defunct football team branded on his flesh. Then I think some more, about the 'set list' in my pocket, and what life the words in the poems will have once they're spoken, whether they'll find a hitching post in someone's memory that could justifiably be thought of as a form of artistic permanence, or simply pop against the eardrum and disappear for ever.

Thirty-nine people constitute a good crowd in the upstairs room of Cafe Irie, a crowd which includes Tony Plant standing at the back, in silhouette. Outside it's pleasantly quiet for a Friday night in such a renowned party town, apart from the low-level beeping and buzzing of the video games and fruit machines in the amusement arcade across the road, and later on the four-letter expletives of half a dozen under-age gamblers being denied access by a doorman built like a bison, a scene I can half see in the corner of my eye. Eventually the reading morphs into a discussion, which feels natural given the intimacy of the setting and the proximity of the audience, though I hadn't expected to be debating the slip roads and service stations of Yorkshire with the obligatory contingent of Tykes who share my interest in moorland motorways and their associated folklore. A woman at the back is keen to tell me that her daughter once submitted a poem of mine as one of her own in a university creative-writing assignment and only got a B. Much laughter in the room.

*

Richard's parents live in St Mawgan, a quiet, largely unspoilt village in the fold of a steep valley within a wooded vale. It's easy to forget there's a military airbase at the top of the road that accommodates civilian passenger flights during the day and more furtive, nocturnal arrivals and departures under cover of darkness and behind the security fence. Richard's mum shows me to the spare bedroom and tells me not to worry if I look out of the window in the morning and see a monk with a strimmer. There's a monastery next door; the brothers tend to keep themselves to themselves but the new abbot is a young American dude with folk-revival facial hair who wears bright-coloured trainers underneath his habit. I walked thirteen miles today but I'm getting to the stage where thirteen miles is something of a stroll, especially when the days are measured by talk rather than distance, and remembered as a landscape of anecdotes and stories rather than stretches of cliff top and views of the sea. There's money in the sock but it sits in the suitcase uncounted and incidental, because the trade-off taking place tonight seems wider and deeper than the ratio of pounds to poems. Twenty-five years ago Richard was a speccy, skinny student writing his dissertation on my work at a time when I'd only published a couple of books and was better known as a probation officer than a poet. He wrote to me out of the blue and I met him in the Albert pub, Huddersfield's equivalent to San Francisco's City Lights bookshop, and bought him a pint and told him everything I knew about poetry, which probably took about half an hour. So if what goes around really does come around, then I guess Richard giving up his bed for the night is a favour returned a quarter of a century later. For which, in return, I feel a peculiar debt of gratitude to my twenty-five-year-old self, a character I probably wouldn't want to spend much time with these days but who on at least one occasion appears to have done someone a good turn. I sink down into the soft mattress, between the cool cotton sheets, and sleep the sleep of the just. The sleep of a monk.

Newquay to St Agnes

Saturday 14 September

It's the morning after the night before and Newquay is regaining consciousness. Someone sweeps broken glass away from a shop doorway. A man loads plastic dustbins of empty bottles into a trailer hitched to his BMW saloon. Someone crawls out from the back seat of a Ford Fiesta, stretches his limbs, cleans his teeth in the corner of the car park with toothpaste and Stella Artois, checks his hair in the wing mirror, then strolls across to the railing overlooking the bay and lights a joint. Jon is setting up tables and chairs on the pavement outside Cafe Irie for would-be breakfasters. I'm sitting on a low wall across the road as the walking party assembles: Charles in a pair of psychedelic shorts, Jo with a camera in her tattooed hands, Peter with a dog called Rufus, and Cornelius, a serious young man from Germany who came to the reading last night and is hoping to publish his PhD based on my work, the eagerly awaited forthcoming best-seller *Mimicking the Universe: Das Verhältnis der Lyrik zur 'Realität' bei Simon Armitage*. 'Sometimes people call me the Colonel,' he says.

Along with yawning and hung-over party-goers the streets of early-morning Newquay are busy with teams of rowers assembling for a gig-racing regatta in the bay. Teams of healthy-faced, muscular young men with all kinds of sail-ing equipment hooked on their arms or hung around their necks are heading downhill in the direction of the water. We're heading uphill, through a housing estate, following Peter, who knows a route to the Penpol footbridge across the Gannel, the best option given that the ferry downstream won't be running for a few hours yet because of the low tide and the Laurie Bridge crossing upstream would put another two miles on today's journey. Penpol is actually a board-

walk leading from one muddy bank to the other, and in Jo's camera lens, with our various shapes and sizes and our idio-syncratic interpretation of what constitutes outdoor wear, we probably look like a pantomime re-enactment of the Beatles traversing the Abbey Road zebra crossing. Rufus takes the direct line through the swampy water then shakes himself dry at the other end, small rainbows forming momentarily where sunlight refracts through the aura of water vapour around his out-of-focus yellow coat.

Bays, coves, inlets, cliffs, porths, the sky, the sea, Tre-this, Tre-that, Tre-the other . . . either I'm becoming so familiar with the day-to-day geography and desensitised to its effects that I'm beginning to take the splendour and beauty for granted, or I'm tired of it, even wearied by its repetitiveness. Or perhaps it's the very richness of the visual experience that I'm starting to react against, as if the extravagance of these seascapes and coastal vistas has made my eyes hungry for something plainer and simpler, something more like the moors of home, and as ungrateful as it seems I find myself glancing inland as often as possible, whenever a gap in the fields opens up or even at a gate in a hedge, looking towards Bodmin and anything else Cornwall has to offer in the way of hills, or just for a horizon that isn't a flat line where the sky rests on the sea. Neither can I muster the necessary enthusiasm when we stop at a house in Holywell for snacks and drinks, but this time it's because we're going so slowly – about one mile an hour by my reckoning, a pace which would see us crawling into St Agnes at about eight o'clock this evening unless someone takes the initiative and ups the pace. Sara and Martin's house is virtually on the beach at the southern end of Holywell Bay, but barricaded from the ocean by a humped sand dune threaded with grasses and reeds. Seated on the decking the Colonel and the rest of the platoon look like they're making themselves comfortable, while I pace around the fenced garden, home to a trampoline, a playhouse, a set of goalposts and a few chickens scratching and pecking at the sandy earth. Sara is going to walk with us but because of a recent injury she's wearing an inflatable pot or splint on her leg, in appearance somewhere between a ski boot and the armoured footwear favoured by clone troopers in the original *Star Wars* film, though hers is in regulation NHS grey, that particularly institutionalised and characterless colour reserved for hospitals, battleships and prisons. She has three such boots, she tells me: one for

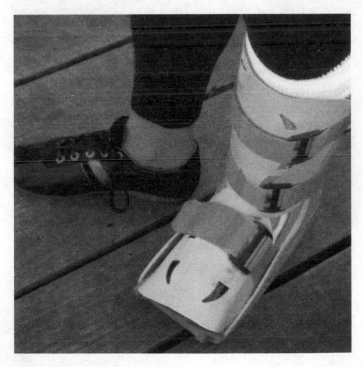

best, one for everyday and one for mucking out the chickens. I don't know which one she's wearing today but it seems inevitable that she might struggle to keep up, and by the time we set out there are nine of us, a straggling Pied Piper parade of adults, children and animals which for all I know might even include a few hens bringing up the rear. On the lane to the beach we become interleaved with a surf-school party heading for the waves, men with the upper halves of their wetsuits rolled down to their waists, partially flensed, or like half-formed creatures still emerging from the tadpole phase. In the way that a kid from the city might describe gang membership or drug addiction, Sara's son describes surfing as an inevitability for young people growing up on the Cornish coast. His dad had a Brummie accent from what I could hear of it between bursts of international rugby union commentary coming from the TV back there at the house, but the son looks and sounds native to these parts, with vowels full of clotted cream. We skirt the fenced military encampment between Penhale and Ligger Point, rows of uninhabited Nissen huts that probably look like a pig farm from spy satellites, and tiptoe around a number of cordoned-off mineshafts on the seaward side of the path, then spill out onto the long yellow length of Perran Beach. As always, getting down on the sand and being close to the waves lifts the spirits and reframes the whole enterprise, though the unending trail of litter and debris along the strandline and scattered generally across the beach punctures any grand notions of being at one with nature. As a protest against such fouling of the oceans, locals have constructed two huge effigies out of washed-up rubbish and sited them on the bank overlooking the beach, a male and

female deity in our own image, made from garbage. The
wheel clamp of Sara's leg brace has proved too much of a
hindrance; half an hour ago she waved a goodbye from the
top of the last headland and headed home with the kids. Jo
and her camera have disappeared as well, so we can kick on
through the tourist town of Perranporth, where a couple
are getting married in a VW camper van, across the concrete slabs of a disused airstrip, past several mineshafts
wearing wrought-iron safety muzzles over their open
mouths, through worked-out quarries smelling of sulphur,
past mineral-rich, ore-infused cliff faces stained with vivid
patches of scarlet, pea-green, cadmium yellow and tanger-
ine, past a bench dedicated to a motorcycle club on a rub-
bled incline hardly negotiable by foot let alone a two-wheeled
vehicle, and finally down the hill and meandering path into
St Agnes, where the figure sitting on the wall in the pub car

park with a beer in his hand and a big grin on his face is Slug.

*

When I walked the Pennine Way, Slug turned up just after the halfway mark with nothing to eat and no idea where we were heading, but begged, borrowed, blagged and breezed his way through three counties, only to pull up just short of Hebden Bridge with a mysterious lameness requiring the kind of medication only provided by a nearby micro-brewery, though he still made it to two further readings courtesy of a cadged ride or a thumbed lift. Thirty years after we first bumped into each other, either in the windowless lecture theatre of Portsmouth Poly's Geography Department, or on the sticky floor of the student union bar, or on the wind-lashed football fields of Southsea's municipal parks and recreation grounds, he's now the friend that I've known for longer than anyone else. And even though in some part of my mind I still think of him as an exotic and unknowable creature whose actions I can never predict and whose private life remains an unexplained and ever-evolving mystery, he's been a constant presence throughout my adult life and across several photograph albums. So while it's a surprise to see him, I would have been disappointed if he hadn't materialised at some stage, not least because of his Cornish ancestry. For my birthday this year and in anticipation of this journey he gave me a leather-bound copy of *The North Coast of Cornwall* by West Countryman John Lloyd Warden Page, published by Joseph Pollard of Truro ('Cornwall! There is a

ring of romance about the very name'), which I've been
dipping into en route, half expecting to be tested on its contents at some stage, Slug priding himself on his geographical, anthropological and antiquarian understanding of the
region. Local accommodation, on the other hand, seems to
lie outside his field of expertise.

'Have you got somewhere to stay tonight?'

'Looking into it, looking into it,' he says, then with an
empty glass in his hand heads back towards the Driftwood
Spars on the other side of the lane for a refill. I go into
Lewsey Lou's fish-and-chip shop to try and offload some of
the coins I've been accumulating over the past couple of
weeks, but the young woman behind the counter clearly has
suspicions about a man who wants to trade several bulging
socks full of loose change for used notes.

'I've just broken into the parking machine,' I say, trying
to defuse the tension with a badly misfiring joke. I feel as if
she's waiting for the correct explanation but there's no way
I'm going to use the word 'poetry' in a fish-and-chip shop,
especially with four or five other people in the queue behind
me now very interested in the outcome of this attempted
transaction.

'I don't think so,' she says after a while, with a beautifully
ambiguous tone that manages to balance both factual information and her personalised reading of the situation. I can
feel myself blushing, as if I'd *been trying it on*, as if I'm some
out-of-town small-time villain hoping to *put one over* on the
unsuspecting locals. Like a con artist, and not a very good
one, foiled in his attempt to scam hard currency from ill-
gotten gains and now dipping into his own pocket to pay for
a meal he didn't really want. In a peevish response to the

rejection my next move is to let a clattering avalanche of bronze and silver come spewing across the counter from the mouth of one of the socks, and to start counting out the cost of cod and chips and a portion of mushy peas, very slowly, beginning with the pennies.

*

There's no one home at the B&B higher up the road but the door isn't locked and there are a few vague written instructions on the back of an envelope on a table in the hall. It's one of those places where the owner's private accommodation and those areas allocated to guests are largely undetermined, or in a continual state of overlap and flux, which almost explains why half an hour later the door of my room flies open and an out-of-breath teenager comes stumbling in. Post-shower, I'm lying on the bed with a towel round my waist reading John Lloyd Warden Page. I look over the top of the book wondering if I'm about to be sexually assaulted or mugged. But before I have time to reach for my holly stick the lad has turned around and gone. About an hour later, now fully clothed and setting off to the reading, I walk past the open door of the living room, where a young couple are rolling around on the floor in each other's arms. When I cough they turn to stare at me but don't get up.

'Is the owner here?'

'No, she's out,' says the young man, who forms the underneath portion of the intertwinement.

'Someone walked into my room,' I say.

'Oh yeah, sorry about that, you're in his bed,' he says.

'Right,' I say. 'Thanks.'

Even before I get to the end of the hallway I can hear that they've resumed their giggling and groping. I nearly turn back to ask for a key, but in this house of freely expressed affection and variable sleeping arrangements it seems unlikely that the outside door will ever be locked.

*

In fact the whole evening is one of misunderstandings and misaligned interactions. The reading gets off to a bad start when I express revulsion at the amount of rubbish strewn along Perran Beach. I mean to pass judgement on the shameful arrogance and embarrassing ignorance of the human race in general but realise almost straight away that it sounds like an accusation of environmental vandalism aimed at local residents. And this in a community famous for its active stance against litter and pollution. I try to dig myself out of the hole but just get deeper and deeper into the sand. I look up at an audience of raised eyebrows and folded arms, and at Slug, who is sitting right in my eye-line trying to suppress a convulsion of laughter. We're upstairs in Schooner's Bistro at Trevaunance Cove, a rectangular-shaped building whose windows look out over the beach and the ocean towards a highly poetic sunset, which is both my backdrop and my competition. Ben, the proprietor, is a wild-haired, wide-eyed man who might be eighteen or might be forty, and is either very laid back or had actually forgotten about tonight's event. In appearance, demeanour and actions he seems to swing between Dylan the Rabbit and Basil Fawlty, one moment telling me that his house is

my house and to make myself at home, the next minute
reseating some puzzled diners to make way for the 'gig' and
turning away late-comers with a wave of the hand. 'Choose
anything you want from the menu and get yourself a drink,
man,' he says. During the reading he keeps emerging from
the staircase at the other end of the room with a confused
expression, as if he's come to investigate that strange, monot-
onous droning sound in the upper storey of his restaurant.
On discovering that the noise is a poetry reading his face
becomes a mask of bafflement and perplexity, before he's hit
by a wave of recognition and recollection, after which he
gives me the thumbs up and descends to the dining room.
With innocent comic timing he appears again at the end of
the question-and-answer session, takes the microphone
from me and asks, 'Right, then, does anyone want to ask
Simon any questions?'

The bar stays open, and it's dark when we leave, Ben saying goodbye with a drink in one hand, a ciggie in the other
and promising a cooked breakfast for anyone who turns up
at eight thirty in the morning. I'd been ignoring it, but the
old undiagnosable aggravation in my hip joints and lower
back has flared up and can be ignored and disguised no
longer, and I have to lean on Slug to get back up the hill.
With my arm around his shoulder we must look like a pair
of drunks heading home from a lock-in, which might be
why the dozen or so men dressed as pirates outside a pub in
the village raise a glass in our direction and shout a loud
pantomimic 'Ouuuu-ahhhhrrrrrr'. In the guest house I can
hear the muffled noise of a TV in another room off the hallway, but no sign of the landlady or the snogging couple. I'm
in too much pain to take off my shoes but still manage to

wedge the Galapagos Tortoise behind the door, remembering that in this house I'm Goldilocks and liable to be surprised by a bear. I need water, painkillers and sleep.

St Agnes to Gwithian

15.5 MILES

Sunday 15 September

No one is surprised that Schooner's Bistro is locked and empty. We peer through the windows to see if Ben's legs are poking out from under the dessert trolley or in case he's flat out on the bar covered by a tablecloth. And we bang on the door a few times, but there's nobody home. It's a particular disappointment for Slug; whichever hostel or manger he slept in last night provided him with a hearty breakfast, but he was hoping that whatever Ben served up could be sur- reptitiously placed between two slices of bread, furtively slipped into a rucksack and brought out later as lunch. Though as he points out, it's perhaps as well that we're leav- ing the village before the arrival of today's edition of the *Western Morning News*, with its banner headline 'Visiting Poet Slams Filthy Cornish', and before locals gather at the top of St Agnes Beacon to pelt me with beach litter.

The Colonel is still in tow, and a couple called Richard and Julie are waiting in the car park dressed in state-of-the- art walking gear, reminding me of something that Charles said yesterday, about sustainability being the clothes you already own, not the latest carbon-neutral socks or anoraks made from recycled floorboards. I have no room to talk: this morning I'm modelling a Sprayway 'softshell' jacket and their most technologically advanced trousers to date, all of which were supplied for free (though after I'd bought all

[216]

the kit I thought I'd need, including the costly miracle hat), with the unspoken understanding that I might give the manufacturer a namecheck, even if a thumbs up from a poet seems like an obscure form of endorsement for an outdoor-clothing brand. And Mammut might not be best pleased to hear that my boots are now more hole than actual footwear, though to be fair they have walked well over a thousand miles without any kind of repair or maintenance, and my wife tells me that a parcel has arrived at home, addressed to me, which could well be replacements. My daughter comes on the line:

The father: 'Do you think they're boots?'

The daughter: 'Could be.'

The father: 'How big's the box?'

The daughter: 'Not small. But not massive.'

The father: 'So is it more like a matchbox, or more like a coffin?'

The daughter: 'Coffin.'

The father: 'Really?'

The daughter: 'But small.'

The father: 'Like for a mouse? Or a rabbit? Or a big dog?'

The daughter: 'I'd say rabbit.'

The father: 'Give it a shake.'

(Sound of small coffin-shaped box being shaken.)

The father: 'Well?'

The daughter: 'Not sure.'

The father: 'Open it.'

The daughter: 'No. Not if it's a dead rabbit.'

I've read about novelists who've entered the compromised world of product placement and have introduced particular brand names into their stories in return for money or merchandise. If I've made the same Faustian pact then so be it, but in a project that's all about bartering and skill swap it feels relevant, even appropriate, and proportionately pitiful in the sense that it's not a Rolex watch or a lifetime supply of Veuve Clicquot but a waterproof cagoule and a pair of lightweight kecks. And some boots, possibly. There's also a sense that I'm putting some of this gear through its paces, though if product *testing* were the objective I might have been better cosying up to one of the pharmaceutical giants, given the number of painkillers and anti-inflammatory pills I've swallowed over the last twenty-four hours. Both my hips feel very sore, as does the small of my back, and I realise I'm walking carefully, suppressing a wince and a grimace when I put added weight on either foot, which is unavoidable in the now customary climb out of the first bay. In an anatomical drawing once scribbled on a notepad by a hospital consultant trying to illustrate my condition, my spine appeared to be the long shaft of a double-headed axe, at the bottom of which the ilium bones formed the two-outward facing blades. At its worst, those two edges feel to be slicing into the cartilage and tendons in my groin every time I move. I've found in the past that the only way of managing the episodes of pain is to rest for a couple of days, ideally in bed. That isn't an option for at least a week, so my strategy is to nurse myself ahead as best I can, and to keep taking the tablets. I tell myself that if I inch cautiously forward without attempting anything too rigorous or abrupt, then I might even *walk it off*, as if steady perambulation might prove to be a form of gentle massage or orthopaedic manipulation. But my spine is reporting a different diagnosis, one of a problem chemically suppressed rather than solved, and a difficulty postponed rather than overcome. Neither is there any let-up in the schedule, two fifteen-mile hikes followed by a seventeen-miler, with Monday and Tuesday involving notoriously rough paths and craggy terrain. The distance doesn't come as a surprise; on one family holiday as a child I sat in the back of my dad's car as we headed towards the West Country, studying the map book, following the journey with my finger along the B roads and trunk roads that were the only routes into the region at the time. With each turn of the page it seemed inevitable that the peninsula would come to an end, but it continued across another double spread, then another, narrowing all the way but pushing onwards and outwards into the sea, even beyond the heel of the Lizard, right to the very last page of the atlas, where the reluctant arched foot of Penwith finally dipped its toe in the Atlantic. The south coast isn't visible yet, but beyond St Agnes there's a definite sense of having entered that spit of land, of travelling along that boardwalk, of walking the plank.

I keep forgetting it's Sunday. Dog-walkers, joggers and families populate the path along the cliff tops, where the grey, drizzly weather seems tailor-made for the derelict engine houses, lifeless chimneys and scarred hillsides of Cornwall's abandoned mining industry. Some of the old shafts are sealed off inside concrete bunkers. Others wear conical-shaped hats made of heavy-duty wire, sieves of a sort, the gauge narrow enough to stop over-inquisitive humans from plummeting to their deaths but wide enough to accommodate the bats which have colonised these man-made caves. We shout our names into one of the shadowy, steamy openings and listen to the muffled echo, and drop pebbles into the darkness to estimate the depth, but no report comes back. Larger stones too are swallowed up by the silence. Sherpas Richard and Julie turned back a few hours ago but have now reappeared up ahead somehow, and a woman who was at the reading in Calstock last week emerges from behind a rock to supply the group with chocolate, though doesn't want to walk with us and holds the confectionery out at arm's length, like a child feeding a horse.

I keep forgetting it's Sunday. After the relative nonevents of Porthtowan and Portreath we find ourselves on a long level path, high above the sea and at times some way back from it, with vehicles in car parks and lay-bys, windscreens facing the ocean, passengers staring towards the rainy horizon. One man in a camper van is partially hidden behind the Travel section of the *Sunday Times*, his feet on the steering wheel and his seat tipped back, oblivious to the weather, the view and to the five of us. In a commendable act of citizenship Slug picks up a wet piece of paper which has become lodged in the side of a hawthorn hedge, only to discover it's a home-printed photograph of a human crotch of indeterminate gender. To throw it away would make him a litter lout but to put it in his rucksack would make him a voyeur or a pervert. What if it inadvertently reemerged at a later date on some family picnic or weekend ramble with friends or colleagues? Caught on the horns of this moral dilemma he carries the image in his hand for the next few miles, looking for a bin and rehearsing excuses just in case we're swooped on by Cornwall Police's counter-pornography division making spot checks along the South West Coast Path.

Beyond the heathland that cushions Navax Point and Godrevy Point, and beyond Godrevy lighthouse, which was Virginia Woolf's eponymous lighthouse and stands sentinel on its own island of rock, and beyond the long arc of bone-coloured sand, fuzzy with sea spray, hemming the semi-circular bay beyond us, St Ives shines in the far distance, white and glimmering, like Jerusalem by the sea. The sea which is frantic and chaotic, driven directly onto the sharp rocks below by a hard, solid wind, leaving the water shredded and annihilated, every part of its surface a fizzing, furious, bright mass of bubbles and froth and spume and spray. Those white horses which have cantered across the steppes of the Atlantic now race each other neck and neck over the last few furlongs, galloping and rising towards the finishing line and hammering into the wall of the coast, vaporising in glittery rainbows of molecules and light. At Godrevy Beach Cafe I eat a slab of cheesecake in order to make the next dose of painkillers part of a balanced meal and to give them a point of anchorage which isn't just the lining of my stomach. We are red-faced, soaking wet, and our table in the corner of the upstairs room is fogged by a microclimate of steam and sweat. Other people are just here for a cup of tea and to read the papers, which is what they do on a Sunday, and I keep forgetting it's Sunday.

*

It is often said that the intensity and clarity of light around St Ives is equal to that of several locations on the French coast where the famous Impressionists painted their work and made their names. Even though it is essentially north-facing the town is clustered around an isthmus, with some parts of it almost entirely surrounded by water, and the bright-coloured houses appear to attract and collect the sea's reflected rays. The light, the air, the relative isolation of the last stop on the train line and the higgledy-piggledy charm of its 'downalong' streets have made it a destination for artists of all kinds over the years, its reputation consolidated by the presence of Ben Nicholson and Barbara Hepworth et al. in the mid-twentieth century and its status cemented (literally, possibly, or maybe concreted) by the opening of Tate St Ives in 1993. Visitors to that gallery can find occasional pieces from the town's rich artistic legacy but more often than not are confronted by touring exhibitions of urban, conceptual or avant-garde work, such as an atrium full of white balloons or a neon sign. In the Hepworth Museum they can peer through the glass at the half-finished structures in the workshop and wonder how such a petite woman from a respectable Yorkshire family wrestled with monoliths of Cornish granite or took on such giant lumps of metal. And along the front and in many of the backstreets they can choose from high-end pots or paintings with 'London prices', watercolours of local landmarks, hand-crafted knick-knacks and mass-produced beach scenes. St Ives, then, is an artists' colony not just in the sense that it offers a home, a community and even an education to many serious practitioners, but that it acts as a point-of-sale to customers of every pocket or purse held captive within the lobster pot of its narrow lanes and cul-de-sac harbour. Whether it's a twenty-thousand-pound red and black abstraction by Sir Terry Frost or a five-quid bit of driftwood with a mermaid painted on it, St Ives is all about the art. So it's right and proper that I'm reading in one of its dozens of galleries, the Porthminster on Westcott's Quay, as part of St Ives September festival. With its four-square granite walls, reinforced porthole windows and wooden storm shutters the building looks as if it forms part of the actual sea defence, with the might of the ocean on one side, priceless paintings, fragile glassware and delicate ceramics on the other, and one trusty slab of stonework in between. Owners David and Dee and gallery manager Claire have gone to a lot of trouble to make the reading happen, creating a seating area on the raised platform to the left of the entrance, welcoming guests with a glass of wine and a tour of the gallery if they want one, and making space among the Bryan Pearces, Peter Lanyons and Sandra Blows to accommodate a travelling poet and his poems. The venue is full to capacity, as defined by health-and-safety regulations, though an extra chair has been squeezed in for Slug, who has been made comfortable with a large Pinot Grigio and a soft cushion. He sits to my right, highly conspicuous and almost part of the event, like a floor manager leading the audience responses with his own highly visible reactions to the poems, or like a prompt ready to supply a line or a couplet if I dry up, and surely he knows every word by now, even the spontaneous ad-libs and off-the-cuff remarks. It's dark when we walk back to a flat at the back of Porthminster Beach, below the railway platform and the stern metal buffer defending the little station and the rest of the town from runaway trains. This is the terminus, although the two red warning lights mounted on a steel frame form an enigmatic colon, suggesting there is more to follow. The painkillers have worn off and I can barely lift one leg to swing it round and put it in front of the other. I thought that sitting for the reading rather than standing would help, but it's made everything worse. Things have seized up. I limp along the path next to the putting green then under the railway tunnel in the manner of a clockwork soldier winding to a halt, and only make it back by holding onto Slug. In the flat I want to vomit with pain but can't bear the agony of getting to my feet again, let alone bending over the toilet. There are only three tablets left in the foil wrap; I've already had more than the recommended daily allowance but I swallow another two and leave the last for morning. I reason that I can face the embarrassment of fail-ing to complete the walk – what choice do I have? – and even honour the arranged readings by getting a ride to the next few destinations, though arriving in a taxi is going to take a lot of explaining, and I can forget about passing around the sock.

*

The tide must be a long way out. And the sea sounds calm and easy, not that industrial push and pull of water against a shingle beach, or even the wheezing and washing of waves on sand. Just a calm shushing, a whispering, a breathing in and a breathing out, a rhythm and length I fall into with my own breath while I'm waiting for the drugs to kick in, while I'm waiting for sleep, replaying the events of the day. Six or seven hours ago we came through the scrubby gorse of Hudder Down, then above the dramatic amphitheatre of Hell's Mouth, well known to birdwatchers and seal-spotters (there's a sign asking visitors to speak quietly so as not to disturb the seals that lay up on the boulders below). A low

safety rail protects part of the rim where the cliff falls away
suddenly and vertically into that terrible crucible, and on
the wrong side of it a young woman was sitting with her
legs dangling over the edge and her eyes on the horizon. We
walked past her and said hello, but she didn't take much
notice of us, and because she wasn't dressed for a walk on
the Coast Path in wet weather, and because there was no
vehicle near by that could have brought her here or could
take her away, and because it was late and she was on her
own, and because it was Hell's Mouth, a site associated not
just with nature lovers but with sad stories and dark inten-
tions, I went back and perched on the rail a couple of yards
away. In a strong Cornish accent she said she was OK, and
didn't want a triangle of Toblerone but thanked me for the
offer. When I asked her if she was *really* OK she told me
that she was, thank you, but that she lost her brother here
about a month ago and had come to sit and remember him
for a few hours. She still wasn't interested in the Toblerone
when I offered it for a second time, or a third, but I didn't
feel as if I could leave without extracting some kind of
promise that she wasn't going to join him, wasn't going to
ease herself over the edge of the cliffs the minute we were
out of sight.

'You're not thinking of doing anything silly, are you?' I
asked.

Such an English thing to say. The patronising, paternal-
istic tone. And the word 'silly': could it be any more trivial-
ising or inadequate? Is there a more insulting epitaph?

'No,' she said, and managed half a smile.

I said, 'And I really can't tempt you with the Toblerone?'

'I'm fine,' she said. 'Honestly.'

A few hundred yards further on we passed a bunch of flowers tied to a fence post, and beneath them an unopened bottle of Betty Stogs beer, and several bike parts such as sprockets and reflectors and a pedal, and a handwritten note saying, 'Arrivederci, Del,' the blue ink smudged by spots of rain.

Earlier in the day we'd witnessed another shrine at the top of the path looking back over Porthtowan. Built into the soil no more than four or five feet from the edge of the cliff it took the form of a miniature garden or model cemetery decorated with carefully positioned pebbles, some with messages and prayers written on them in white paint. The eye then followed an inch-wide path that curled through the tended mound of stones and earth, past a carved cross, past a carefully arranged bunch of red and yellow flowers towards a little stick or cane with a miniature glitter ball hanging from its hook, spinning and swaying in the breeze. To the left of the flowers, the towers of a child's fairy-tale palace reached into the air, each green plastic turret flying a pink satin banner or flag. I crawled around the back of the shrine on hands and knees to look down onto the rocks, but didn't even get to the edge, because the fall was too far to contemplate.

Gwithian to Zennor

Monday 16 September

We get a taxi to Gwithian so we can pick up where we left off. I've popped my last pill and am hobbling forward. If I make it back to St Ives I'll have to make a decision about whether I'm fit enough to carry on, or I could go in search of a prescription and a dispensing chemist.

It's just me and Slug today. There have been times on this walk and other walks when I've felt as if his meanderings and dawdling have held me up. He takes things at an easier pace than I do, doesn't share the same sense of urgency, and yet if I hadn't had his shoulder to lean on or his gags to laugh at these past couple of days I might have packed in by now. I should probably thank him, but he wouldn't hear me because the wind on Gwithian Beach is coming off the sea with such ferocity and volume that it's impossible to communicate other than with sign language. Around the entire horseshoe of the bay there isn't another person in sight, until a lone windsurfer comes flashing past, the blue sickle of his sail yanking him yards into the air so he appears to be flying for seconds at a time, and when he turns diagonally to tack and jibe the other way he's a rodeo rider, the surfboard bucking and kicking beneath him, the high waves trying to flip him base over apex, yet somehow he stays upright. A little further on we pass the Reggie Perrin-style heap of his clothes laid on a towel: a pair of shiny leather shoes, grey trousers, an ironed white shirt, a black jacket and a rolled-up blue tie poking out of the breast pocket. A gale hurtles in. We're blasted by rain, then sand-blasted, then pelted with rain again, rain that arrives horizontally, a flack of small hard droplets that might even be hailstones. They sting the hands and the cheeks, and when I pull the drawstring that tightens my hood around my face they spit and ping against the shiny nylon fabric. Slug has gone down to the shoreline to take photographs but is beaten back by the weather, and for the next ten minutes or so it's like the opening scenes of *Saving Private Ryan*, rounds of rain fizzing past, a booming, banging wind, and nowhere to hide on the exposed shore. Then just as quickly as it came the rain goes flapping away over the sandbanks, and the wind settles, and the beach is now a flat, quiet place, with one herring gull standing on a protruding rock in the middle of a shallow lagoon, and about a dozen oystercatchers in parade-ground formation between here and the sea, their comical orange beaks all pointing the same way. We walk through a sandy gorge between barnacle-encrusted outcrops, and two skewbald horses gallop into view, sending the oystercatchers scrambling and trumpeting skywards. Both riders are female: one has a long blonde ponytail that mimics the bouncing and flicking of the tail of the horse beneath her, and the other wears a pink equestrian helmet. The rain rushes in again then rushes out. Four turnstones play chicken with the tide. At the far end of the bay, where the rim of white sand narrows to a point and in a mirage of morning sun, St Ives looks like a model town made from pebbles and shells.

For someone who lives about as far away from the sea as it's possible to get in Britain, I have an inexplicable number of poems about bodies of water, and the perils of crossing them, and the dangers of falling into them. Last night I read 'Causeway', about a near-drowning on the land bridge between Marazion and St Michael's Mount. And I read 'The Strid', about the notorious 'crossing point' on the River Wharfe near Bolton Abbey, where the water enters a narrow, rocky channel. At various times in history and in various moments of myth people have attempted to jump over the Strid, usually with fateful consequences. Wordsworth wrote about it in his poem 'The Force of Prayer', describing how Young Romilly cleared the Strid in one bound but his reluctant greyhound pulled him back with the leash. Man and dog fell into the fast-running current and were drowned. Some years ago it was reported in the press that a pair of newlyweds had apparently attempted a similar leap, and with the same tragic outcome. Their bodies were carried downstream and hauled out of the water several days later. And I read my poem 'Song of the West Men', about Guðlaugur Friðþórsson, whose trawler capsized in the cold seas off the south-west coast of Iceland in 1984. Against all the odds, and aided by his blubbery body mass, he survived in the water for over six hours and eventually made landfall on the treacherous volcanic rocks of the Westmann Isles. He broke through a crust of ice to drink water from a sheep trough, then walked along the dirt road towards the lights of his home town of Heimaey, where locals were dumbfounded by his miraculous, bare-footed return. In my balladic telling of his story he becomes a kind of Christ figure, returning from the dead. Those three poems and others on the same watery theme were on my mind in anticipation of today's leg of the journey, which involves either the crossing of the River Hayle or a very long and unrewarding walk around the Hayle Estuary, much of it next to a busy road. Like the Strid, many people – usually holidaymakers – have come a cropper at the mouth of the Hayle, usually attempting to wade or swim from Porth Kidney Sands to The Towans. My cousin's daughter was a lifeguard on that beach and has talked about the dangers of the current, and how swiftly the river disgorges into the sea, even at low tide, when the watercourse looks little more than a placid stream. With that in mind, and to save me a long and boring slog inland, the Cornish wing of my family have very kindly offered to meet me on the sandy riverbank and paddle me across in their kayak, a trip of no more than twenty or thirty yards. But by Black Cliff there's no sign of them, and no sign of them further upstream, and no reply to my texts and no one answering their phone. Standing at the water's edge, looking into the hazy, wobbling depths, we begin to think the unthinkable, and go as far as untying our boots, pulling off our socks, rolling up our trouser legs and taking a step off the edge. But even at a depth of just six or seven inches I can feel the drag of the water tugging at my foot, and if the rate of flow isn't enough of a deterrent the temperature certainly is, like a cast of ice from my ankle downwards, a strange mixture of numbing anaesthetic and intolerable discomfort. We dry off and begin the trudge to the south, all the way past the locked containers of Hayle Canoe Club, through a deserted industrial estate, along the esplanade and under the viaduct, along the narrow pavement with cars and lorries roaring past in both directions, around the head of the marsh with the sound of rainforest parrots and other exotic birdlife carried downwind from Paradise Park Wildlife

Sanctuary, alongside the railway line at Lelant Saltings, through a lychgate and graveyard and a golf course and under a bridge, until we're back where we were an hour and a half ago give or take a Strid or two, on the other side of the channel. But dry and alive.

It's well past midday, St Ives is still some distance away and Zennor is six or seven miles beyond St Ives along an infamously rough path. The pampas grass and palm trees are becoming taller and more frequent as we wander through Carbis Bay, and the garden of one bungalow boasts a profusion of tropical cacti. At a high point above St Ives, in a clearing between roofs and trees, what looks like a whitewashed bus stop is actually the Baulking House, 'a Huer's lookout from which watch was kept for shoals of pilchards in the bay and the movements of the seine boats were directed'. I've seen a photograph of Porthminster Beach where no sand is visible because of the number of fishing boats waiting there at low tide, and Virginia Woolf once remarked that the smell of fish in the town was so strong it stopped the church clock. But there's no pilchard industry here any more, just 'grockles' and 'emmets', and as we funnel into St Ives proper along the rat run of the Warren we have to weave our way through tourists in swimming costumes and sun hats criss-crossing between the town's several beaches. Slug queues up for veggie pasty and I go in search of an apothecary. Ideally I'd spend a few hours here, take in the Tate and the harbour, but even Slug seems to appreciate that if we're going to get to Zennor before sundown, we need to shift. The only place we dawdle is in the cemetery, looking for the grave of Alfred Wallis, the local naïve painter whose cause was taken up by Ben Nicholson and whose childlike solution to problems of perspective, distance and scale was to pretty much ignore them. The grave is hardly inconspicuous but appropriately innocent, Bernard Leach tiles showing an enormous lighthouse with a tiny cartoon seafarer at its base, and no headstone. 'INTO THY HANDS O LORD'. We add a couple of white pebbles from the path to the several contributed by other visitors, pebbles which sit like counters on an arcane board game, and move on, past the wind-knotted holly tree growing out of the corner of the plot.

Near Clodgy Point, after the town, there's a granite waymarker carved with the words 'St Ives to Zennor', but the mileage has been eroded by the weather or chipped off by human hand. From here, Cornwall falls away to the west and south, never to reach this latitude again, always bending out of view to its far tip, and to tread further is to enter a landscape ancient and primitive in atmosphere and appearance, different to any that has gone before, beyond the end of the regular tourist trail, a place that many uphold as beautiful and beguiling but which to my eye is forbidding and not a little sinister. This isn't to pass comment on its inhabitants: there aren't many of them anyway along this curving, dipping, cornering edge of Britain, and the fact that there isn't a seaboard community of any size until Sennen Cove, just a few miles before Land's End curls its nose up at the Atlantic, suggests that others have found it equally unwelcoming. It's more about the geography and the geology: the coastline of infinitely squiggly bays and coves, the sharp rocks both above and below the water line, the cottages perched on precipitous eyries or cowering behind headlands, and the complex jigsaw pattern of tumbledown walls enclosing unfeasibly small fields whose main crop appears to be stones. All this on a peninsula that suffers everything the shipping forecast areas of Fastnet, Fitzroy and Sole can muster and unload. The path echoes those themes, the next four or five miles of it being boggy and steep, and where stones do occur underfoot they lie at angles other than the horizontal, providing trip hazards, ankle traps, slippery surfaces, sharp edges and every kind of obstacle and hindrance, until it's impossible to know whether to walk on them and risk breaking a bone or walk around them and risk immersion in mud or falling down a mineshaft or crashing onto those horrible rocks to the right which form a cruel-looking fortification around every inlet and bay. The land here resists incursion, repels intrusion. It's awkward, stubborn, and doesn't yield quietly to foot or wheel, to plough or spade, to the approach of rudder or prow. What paths exist are hard won and easily lost. Everywhere is craggy, mangled, wizened. In other words, my back hurts like never before. Do I have to spell it out?

Slug wins a bet to see the first seal of the day. The thrashing breakers pound and slam against the coruscating rocks, but after every detonation of water the seal re-emerges through bubbling whiteness, nosey and unconcerned. Beyond Mussel Point, that furry thing up ahead is a microphone in a windsock, and the person holding it, wearing headphones clamped against his ears, is Tim, who has come to record me reading a few Charles Causley poems to be broadcast on the tenth anniversary of Causley's death. Tim walked with me on the first day, to Porlock Weir from Minehead, and in the time it's taken me to get this far he's been to Zambia and back. Striding towards me with a suntanned face and a big grin it's as if he's orbited the whole world while I've been plodding along this coast. He tells me that he'd almost given up on me, and I tell him that's fair enough because I'd almost given up on myself. A posse of teachers and students from Truro High School are waiting in ambush around the next bend. Afterwards I can't remember if we circumnavigate Zennor Head or cut the corner and make straight for the village, which is a very annoying half a mile from the pre-scribed route. I get the drinks in and Slug makes enquiries about a bed for the night at the Tinner's Arms. And a sherpa for his luggage. And a lift to the reading tonight. And a lift back to the pub later on. It's a routine I recognise by now, how he openly and in front of as many people as possible states the nature of his logistical paradox, scratches his head, then waits until the silence is broken by someone volunteer-ing their services as either a driver, a courier service, a cook or a landlord, and preferably all four. And there is *always* a volunteer. He also adopts a particular facial expression, which I've always thought of as having 'puppy dog eyes', but which on this occasion are the eyes of a seal. A seal cub. Orphaned, and washed up on a beach.

*

A man called Mav is looking for me.

'What's Mav short for?'

'Maverick.'

We drive for about twenty minutes in his Peugeot fast-back, roaring along narrow lanes and bumpy surfaces better suited to tractors or four-wheel drives. I like to think of myself as the possessor of a good inner compass but readily admit by the time we arrive at Bodrifty Farm that I've no idea where we are or in which direction we've travelled, and this on a strip of land only a handful of miles wide. We seem to be quite high up, on a moor maybe, but not above the tree line. We turn down a drive, blocked for a few minutes by a farmer who's doing something important with a herd of cows and is being assisted or impeded by two young blond boys who are swinging on fences and banging wooden sticks on the ground. A lady called Penny appears and walks at the side of the car all the way along the drive, talking to me through the open passenger window, though I can't hear a word because of the car's throaty exhaust. Penny marshals us past a log shed stacked with seasoned wood and into a lawned glade, then Emma takes over, leading me into a circular wooden cabin with its own toilet, sitting area and kitchenette, and where a literal smorgasbord of posh cheeses, unusual spreads and high-end snacks are set out on the worktop. The building looks as if it might have been constructed around a living tree, like Odysseus' bed.

'Alright for you?'

'Fantastic.'

'Any questions?'

'Er . . . is there . . . where do I sleep?'

I'm expecting Emma to pull down a spring-loaded platform from the roof space or make a mattress unroll from the armchair, but instead she points across the lawn to a structure that looks like the love child of a circus tent and a toadstool, or a yurt crossed with a wigwam, a massive fairytale roundhouse with a conical thatched roof sweeping down to a low, circular wall of big granite blocks, with a wide doorway under its cropped fringe barred by an impressive wooden door.

'You sleep in there,' she says.

It's dark inside, under the ribs of the roof beams, and largely empty apart from an absolutely enormous four-poster bed. Aromatic wood burns in a metal fire bowl in the middle.

'And where's the reading?'

'In here.'

'On the bed!' I say, jokingly.

'Yes,' says Emma.

Back in the cabin I prepare my reading, while Emma uncorks a bottle of wine and drinks it, chatting away about the history of this Iron Age site, and how her dad, Fred, renovated the farmhouse then built the roundhouse and the other structures on site. She has what sounds like a London accent and a vocabulary that suggests an exciting past. The family own about fifty acres of this ancient, historic countryside, and let the various buildings out to tourists with a taste for something out of the ordinary.

*

By seven thirty owls are hooting in the surrounding woods and people are arriving for the event, Penny directing them across the paddock towards the roundhouse, which in the fading light now looks like a disembodied witch, the pointy hat of the roof rising above the horizon, the open door alive with the glow of candlelight like a big cackling mouth. The audience are sitting two or three deep in ripple formation, the ripples emanating from the huge four-poster. I can't bring myself to actually read in the prone position, propped up on pillows – it's just too perverse. Instead I hitch up onto the foot of the bed, perch on the end of the mattress and begin my introduction. The bed isn't just wide, it's also absurdly high; sitting under the canopy, between the pulled-back drapes, with my legs dangling over the edge and not reaching the floor, I must look like an elf about to recite from a book of spells or charms. Fred, who is a man of few words, obviously did his homework on the subject of planetary alignment because the moon gradually appears in the doorway, perfectly framed by the upright timbers, not quite a full moon but not far off, and one that stares silently and attentively like another face in the crowd. But Fred's understanding of fire and its various by-products is, in my opinion, less thoroughly researched. After ten minutes, even with the door fully open, it's apparent to everyone that the roundhouse – which has no chimney or even a hole in the roof – is filling up with smoke. He steps forward to waft a bit of air onto the smouldering logs, to make them burn hotter and cleaner, but this intervention only serves to drive the smoke further into the room and to propel a constellation of sparks in the direction of the bed and upwards into the thatch. The majority of the audience are obviously in some discomfort but are too polite to leave, and sit there coughing and spluttering between poems, rubbing their eyes and inhaling fumes. At least three people are using the sleeves of their jumpers as breathing masks. I rush towards the end, getting hoarser and more croaky with every sentence, and reckon there's just time for a couple of questions before people begin to expire.

'Can't you speak up?' asks a lady near the back.

I say to her, 'I'm really sorry, but I've walked about two hundred and fifty miles to get here. Couldn't you just drag your cushion about ten feet this way?' And with that acrid comment mingling with the smoke in the room the reading comes to an end. Everyone hurries outside to take a deep drag of the clear evening air.

*

From the wooden cabin the silhouette of the roundhouse is still just about visible against the starlit sky. The moon has taken its leave, but the fire bowl glows like a big red eye in the middle of the field, dragged outside after the event and left to die down in its own time. Half an hour ago I'd mounted the bed again and shuffled under the sheets, but couldn't get to sleep. It wasn't just the fumes, although there was a slight sense of being kippered overnight in a smokehouse and a fear of those sparks finally coming to life in the highly combustible roof during the small hours, setting the whole place alight with me in the middle, the fire brigade finding me three days later in the dying embers like a baked hedgehog. The real reason was extreme self-consciousness, a sense of being one tiny person in a gigantic bed and a lone human being in an empty, cavernous space, like an ant under a tureen. A feeling of heightened conspicuousness, despite there being no one else around, and a desire for the nearness of furniture and ceilings and walls. That's why I descended from the double-decker four-poster bed and crossed the lawn, trying to keep the duck-down duvet and Egyptian cotton sheets from dragging in the dew. And that's why I'm taking a last look at the roundhouse through the cabin window before brushing my teeth and curling up in a nest on the floor, comforted by the purring of the fridge and the proximity of a chair, feeling myself proportionate to this space, equal to its shape, on level terms with its height, width and depth.

Legends of the Crossings

One man conquered the estuary's swell
in a scallop shell
that had served as an ash tray,
another canoed on a fallen ash tree.
One woman crossed in the dimpled sloop
of an ice-cream scoop,
or was it soup ladle
with a butter-knife rudder and teaspoon paddle?
Two surfer dudes rolled in from abroad
surfing ironing boards.
Fused at the hip, conjoined twins
rode shotgun on the pectoral fins
of a freshwater porpoise;
a willing Galapagos tortoise
ferried their oversize luggage bank to bank.

A cockler sank
then rose then sank then rose and rose
on the whiskery tip of a grey seal's nose.
Some Michael rode
his boat ashore, some Jesus strode
the unwalkable ford, a widow scattered
her husband's ashes
into the raging burn
then wobbled home in the empty urn,
and a jilted bride
forged a perfectly good flotation device
from her ex-fiancé's everyday lies,
which were watertight.
A church cross, hewn from a single dogwood trunk
was raft enough for a bearded monk:
a marooned shipmate simply waited
for winter, then simply skated.
Fleeing dune to dune,
a refugee played a comical tune
on the xylophonic stepping stones
of a dead whale's bones,
and a saintly young thing voyaged land to land –
get this – in her own cupped hand
and didn't sink.
But look, our pedestrian stalls at the salty brink
with his waterproof hat and holly stick
and chickens out. He bottles it.

Zennor to Land's End

Tuesday 17 September

Emma is up early. I was hoping to sneak the bedding back to the roundhouse this morning before anyone woke up, to avoid getting into any complicated justification of my nocturnal activities. But she spotted me crossing the lawn carrying the sheets on my head like a big, badly wrapped turban. In an outdoor coat, a nightie and a pair of wellies she walks into the cabin at just after seven and begins making coffee.

'How come you didn't sleep over there?'

'It was too strange,' I say. 'Like sleeping in a tagine.'

'Freaked you out, did it? I was in the woodshed,' she says, without explanation, helping herself to some breakfast. She chats away while I cram everything into the Galapagos Tortoise and drag it towards the door.

'Who was that mate of yours last night?'

'Slug.'

'What kind of name's that?'

'His surname's Slegg. It's Cornish. He spends a lot of time down here.'

'He can stay with us if he helps out a bit.'

'I think he did a bit of dry-stone walling once but to be honest he's more of a party animal than a farmhand.'

'I'm sure we can find him a job as a gimp.'

*

Mike and Jane pick me up. Mike is a dentist and is having the day off. Jane is ferrying the Galapagos Tortoise to Cape Cornwall then rendezvousing with us at Land's End later in the day. Slug, who cajoled the landlord at the Tinner's into taking him to the reading last night and collecting him afterwards, is nowhere to be seen. In the Mary Celeste of his room there's a pile of his clothes on the floor, an empty pint pot on the bedside table, a whiff of his deodorant in the air and the impression of his body in the bed sheet, but no Slug. Acting on a hunch I shout his name into the foggy grave-yard of Zennor Church, and a few moments later he emerges from behind a tombstone with a camera around his neck. Quarter of an hour later we're about ready to set off, but not until he's talked Jane into transporting his suitcase for him.

'Where are you staying tonight?'

'I don't know, really. I suppose I'll just have to hope there's a vacancy somewhere in Penzance or Newlyn,' he says, rais-ing his hands in sorrowful appeal and looking towards her with a pained expression that can only be healed by someone with a motorised vehicle, a spare duvet and an empty place at their table. A silence follows, broken eventually by Mike with the offer of the en suite guest bedroom at their house, plus a lift to and from the reading tonight plus breakfast in the morning.

'Well,' says Slug, 'as long as it's no trouble.'

*

We're joined at the last moment by a woman whose name I don't catch but who might be another Jane, and set off down a gulley with grotesque ear-trumpets of gunnera burgeoning at the side of a stream. I can barely believe it, but my back seems better today, which I put down to sleeping on the floor last night rather than in the Great Bed of Ware with its bouncy castle of a mattress and its Bayeux Tapestry of a quilt cover and its cumulonimbus pillows, from which I might never have returned. The forecast today is rain, followed by more rain, followed by heavy rain, and so far it is proving reliably accurate. The path is onomatopoeic with sticky mud and squelchy soil, though the sea is calmer than usual. Not the constant thundering and crashing timpani of yesterday, more the slow, rhythmic inhalation and exhalation of a piano accordion played in a downstairs room. Gurnard's Head is visible, the protruding blob of land whose profile is said to resemble the eponymous marine animal itself, though I can't comment on the accuracy of the analogy because I don't believe I've ever seen a gurnard and fish silhouettes have never been a strong subject for me. I've been offered a free pint in the pub on the horizon named after the same creature, but there isn't time.

*

This is one of those days when any concept of dryness has to be left behind. For the most part the summer has behaved itself, fallen in with traditional meteorological expectations. In some ways it's been a rose-tinted *old-fashioned summer*, an anachronistic reminder of what the climate was like before the glaciers started to melt and sea levels began to rise and storm clouds gathered on the horizon, the days before the position of the jet stream figured in our conversations or became a regular feature of the evening weather bulletin.

And like all traditional and nostalgic summers, this one has come to its teary and lachrymose conclusion towards the middle of September, with bouts of weeping culminating in an episode of inconsolable sobbing which looks set to last for the foreseeable or at least forecast-able future. After only an hour, and despite many layers of high-performance, breathable and waterproof fabrics, I'm not just wet, I'm marinated, stewing in a slimy brew of condensation, sweat and rain. My boots feel like two buckets of swamp water and are now being held together by pink bailing twine threaded through the eyelets and looped under the heel, the laces having perished and the uppers having parted company with the soles. Even though I'm not wearing glasses I feel fogged up by internal mist, and ahead on the path the three others appear shrouded in steam. Near Robin's Rocks we pause to admire mighty breakers battering the coastline. Slug says he's read about mineshafts that extend for miles under the seabed, and that during violent storms miners could hear the rolling and bumping of giant boulders above them on the ocean floor, though the woman who might be Jane disputes the authenticity of the tale and puts it down to legend and lore.

As per most days on this walk it's tiring on the feet and tiring on the eye, keeping to the narrow vein of the track which turns without warning and is studded with awkward and irregular rocks poking out of the earth, and having to watch the heels of the person in front for miles at a time with no real view to either side other than the vague greenish blur of the land to the left and the vague bluish smear of the sea to the right. By Pendeen it's so gloomy and misty that we can't see the lighthouse at all, only hear an unsettling lowing noise like someone blowing across the top of a milk bottle or running a wet finger around the rim of a bowl, but without being able to say which direction the sound is coming from. Slug reckons it's a sound-buoy about half a mile off the coast, but the woman who might be Jane says it isn't. We have to trust to the path when it feels to be tacking in the wrong direction or heading towards danger. Two or three times I find myself thinking of Arthur Machen's 'ghost story' 'The White People', a story I read when I was seventeen after hearing it described as 'the scariest thing ever written'. It isn't scary. There are no dead bodies and none of the usual tricks or tropes associated with the genre. But it is unsettling, an unresolved tale within a tale within a tale of a child's wanderings across dreamlike, pagan countryside, past haunting landmarks and primitive stone structures, to where something or someone waits, where some highly significant but almost ineffable experience takes place. No film version of the book could ever be properly realised, but as a potential

location this stretch of the Cornish coast seems ready-made, especially as we enter the deserted and desecrated mining landscape around Geevor and Levant and the Crown. A ghoulish tourist trail has grown up around the now defunct industries of tin, lead and copper extraction, but the tea rooms, museums and car parks are invisible in this all-enveloping pea-souper, and the day-trippers non-existent, leaving us to stumble alone past the tumbledown engine houses and muted chimneys that have the look and feel of an enterprise abandoned almost overnight. Where the ground has been brutalised and hacked nature has been slow to mend the wounds and heal the scars. Columns that once supported the roofs of outbuildings and sheds stand like petrified beings, post-apocalyptic, fixed in time. Rock faces ooze with stream water and the earth bleeds rust. Steps lie crooked and broken among gouged soil and spoil heaps of shale. It's unusual and possibly even unique on this walk to experience a landscape which is so man-made, and entirely unexpected given the remoteness of the location. At times it's reminiscent of Pompeii or the Palatine area of Rome, the decaying ruins and rubble of a once busy, once thriving community, the proof and evidence of human activity come to a sudden halt, though without the illuminating and animating Italian sun to bring the past to life. This place looks finished. Dead. In fact strip away the Cornish romance and the Celtic sentimentality and this could be a war zone or the post-Thatcher coalfields of South Yorkshire, and who would want to holiday there?

My dad phones up. I tell him that I'm getting close to the end, and when he says, 'I think this will be your last long walk,' it's less of an observation and more of an instruction, issued partly out of a concern for my skeletal structure and partly as a response to increased childcare duties over these past three weeks. We stop for lunch and Slug produces the potato, sweetcorn, carrot, swede and pea pasty which has been fermenting at the bottom of his rucksack since St Ives, the rucksack which he has been using as a backrest and a cushion. In its compacted and dehydrated state the pasty looks like roadkill on a busy dual carriageway after a bank-holiday weekend.

*

Cape Cornwall comes into view. Slug says it's the only place in England with the word 'Cape' in its name, though I quibble with him, pedantically, citing Scapegoat Hill above Golcar, west of Huddersfield, as another example. I used to play football for the pub team there, the Scape House, getting changed in the cellar among the barrels and pumps then jogging up to the 'ground', which was really a cow field with a few white lines drawn on it and a pair of parallelogram goals pushed out of perpendicular alignment by the wind. It was the highest and most exposed place for hundreds of square miles, with views as far as Humberside to the east and with Pennine gales crashing in from the west. About a third of our home games were called off every season, either because of storms, or thick fog, or concerns about lightning, or drifting snow even as late as Easter, and once because of frozen molehills. There's a similarly incongruous sporting venue around this headland in the shape of Cape Cornwall Golf Club, signalled by a blue flag which breaks the horizon above a bracken-filled valley bridged by a tombstone-sized slab of granite. The implausibly steep fairways climb or plunge towards the lurid oases of the greens. Standing imperiously above golf course, valley, cape and Atlantic Ocean is Porthlodden House, home of the Physick family, a colossal construction made more conspicuous by its isolation and elevation, and my lodgings for the night. I call in to see Tara, who is mucking out the horses, then catch up with the others at the bottom of Cot Valley, where we edge around the valley mouth to witness the thousands of circular boulders of varying size half buried in the cliff face, bulging from their sockets, some like popping eyes, some like embedded embryos or eggs about to hatch. Then we fail to spot newts in what Mike says is the most westerly newt pool in England, despite staring hard into the soupy green depths and parting the long straggly weeds with our hands.

*

Do people tell me preposterous things so that in ignorance and innocence I'll write them in my book? Was Mike really one of a party who encountered an escaped vulture perched on a rock in Whitesand Bay, and did he really see someone stroll right up to it and feed it a sandwich? Had it really circled the peninsula for two or three days beforehand, running out of energy, running out of land, before being captured and provided with retirement accommodation in Paradise Park bird sanctuary? Did those Cornish people under its shadow really see it as an omen of their imminent demise? More believable is his explanation for the chunks of hard orange foam like cinder toffee on the beach, from the spilt cargo of a ship carrying thousands of car dash-

boards which broke up on the rocks. The sea here is entirely white with froth and fizz, roused and brought to the boil
where the prevailing current lashes out for one last time at
the trailing promontory of land before dividing either side
of Britain's south-west tip. The wind has made flame-
throwers of two red flags speared in the sand, and a pair of
lifeguards in their hut halfway up the bank at the back of
the bay tell us we're the first people they've seen all day.
Land's End, a theme park for some, for others the terminus
of a long quest, is meaningless to me when I arrive at about
three in the afternoon and pose for pictures under the signposts and mileage fingers pointing to John O'Groats and
New York, next to the exhibition centre and the 4D cinema
and the interactive Arthurian experience and the petting
zoo. I see it only as a stepping-off point and a compass bearing in the direction of Longships lighthouse and its retinue
of sharp rocks just about visible where the sea and the sky
bleed into each other in a coming together of mist and
spray, and to the invisible islands beyond.

*

Newlyn School of Art have reserved a parking place for me
with a piece of cardboard bearing my name tied to a metal
dustbin. I get out of Tara's car and drag it to one side. The
building is a former Victorian schoolhouse in Newlyn's
'artists' quarter' and the car park is the old playground.
The audience is already seated and waiting when I arrive.
I read in front of the high windows to about a hundred
people. Afterwards there's an exhibition to look around in
an old fish factory at the bottom of the hill, with paintings

and artworks housed in all kinds of spaces from the cold
store to the rafters, all inspired by my poems apparently,
but there isn't enough time to take it all in or be properly
grateful. Porthlodden House feels like another gallery
when we get back there, with more Cornish art hanging
from the walls than I've seen in any other building anywhere, including Tate St Ives. I'm taken on a tour of rooms,
corridors and halls, some dedicated to specific artists or
movements, with famous images hanging framed and
spotlit. When the tour concludes it's late and dark, and the
final masterpiece is the slither of twilight beyond the
remains of St Helen's Chapel on the knob of land in front
of the great window at the top of the grand staircase, looking west. Or is the sun the moon?

Penzance to St Mary's

Wednesday 18 September

Today is the longest journey but the shortest walk, two hundred yards at most from the passenger seat of Tara's car to
Penzance Quay. The passenger check-in is a small Portakabin containing a man and a clipboard. He opens the little
window, runs his finger up and down his list of names, then
points in the direction of the only ship in the harbour. I've
ditched the Galapagos Tortoise, left it at an address on the
Cornish mainland to be collected at some unspecified date,
and with it most of my books, having folded a sheaf of
photocopied poems into my top pocket for the readings
ahead. If I'm short of material I'll have to hope that at least
one person on that outlying cluster of granite rocks has at
least one of my slim volumes that I might be able to borrow
for an hour, or I'll have to improvise. I've cast aside my broken footwear as well, left the remains suppurating and bio-
degrading in the porch of Porthlodden House, at the end of
a long line of green wellies and riding boots, like a couple of
clapped-out bangers in the car park at Ascot next to a fleet
of Range Rovers and other luxury all-terrain vehicles. But
I've gained a Sue. She arrived by magic, out of the night, the
bringer of northern gossip and comfortable shoes. I woke
up next to her this morning in the big white raft of the bed
in the big-windowed bedroom looking out over earth and
sea, so for a few minutes before breakfast we were King and

Queen of Cape Cornwall surveying our province from the balcony, overseeing the world through the thinning, sun-dyed gauze of morning mist. From now on I'm travelling happy and light.

Unprofitable helicopter flights to the Scillies have ceased operating of late, and flights from Land's End Airport (a field near St Just) are prone to cancellation when the grassed airstrip becomes waterlogged or when sea fog shrouds the peninsula, and it's rumoured that the light aircraft which shuttles back and forth (a sort of canoe with wings) won't depart unless the islands are actually visible to the pilot. It means the *Scillonian III* is by far the most dependable means of transport, the Appledore-built ferry making the three-hour crossing every day, providing a vital link to the mainland for the Scillies' two thousand and some population and bringing in all the commodities and raw materials necessary to sustain life and lifestyle, the most valuable being tourists. Despite being fitted with an anti-rolling device to compensate for its shallow draught the ship is notoriously 'sloppy' in many senses of the word, a floating vomitorium in fact, sometimes referred to as 'the big white stomach pump'. Residents of Hugh Town sometimes stroll down to the pier to watch green-faced passengers come staggering ashore, apparently, and I notice that the pouch pockets in the back of the wipe-down seats in the 'lounge' offer not one but several sick bags per person. Following seagoing advice from all kinds of sources, most of it contradictory, we find a forward-facing bench on the outside, upper deck, stare at a fixed point on the horizon and swallow mouthfuls of fresh air. Many of our fellow travellers appear to be bird-watchers, solitary middle-aged men in shower-proof beige trousers and RSPB fleeces with rucksacks on their backs and binoculars around their necks, who suddenly lift the glasses to their eyes to track some near-invisible speck of white flying a few yards above the surface of the water at great speed and at great distance. They follow up this action with a pencilled entry in a small notebook which is produced then returned to a breast pocket with a fluency of habit perfected over several decades. A naturalist-in-residence standing at the aft of the ship helpfully points out John le Carré's house on the hillside near Mousehole, then reels off an inventory of creatures spotted from this very vessel on recent journeys, including gannet, Arctic skua, Leach's petrel, kittiwake, fulmar, Manx shearwater, leatherback turtle and even minke whale. To his checklist of wildlife he might also add the shell-less gastropod mollusc more commonly known as Slug, who emerges from below deck with open arms and a broad grin on his face. Slug, of the Slegg family. Or, on a romantic island getaway such as this one, sometimes referred to as a gooseberry.

The going gets rough beyond the sheltering, protective arm of Cornwall, out on the open sea where currents and winds compete and collide. The boat slews and rolls, jerking and pitching particularly vigorously at about the halfway stage, above what some believe to be the sunken Arthurian domain of Lyonesse. At the two-hour mark all conversations have petered out and many aboard are sitting with their eyes closed or their vision locked to the lands up ahead, not at all a discernible pattern of identifiable islands as they seemed on the map but an apparently swirling and rotating orrery of shapes and forms with no obvious port or settlement to steer for. Only a contemporary monk appears untroubled by the heaving of the seas and the hurling of the ship. Bearded, bespectacled, in a knee-length habit tied with a hemp rope, he stands amidships, hands behind his back and with no need of support, a kind of holy surfer buoyed by faith and steadied by belief, his bare hairy legs solidly planted in a pair of black Nike Tiempo trainers with a gold tick on the side.

The ticket for the ferry crossing was a barter, in exchange for a reading at Five Islands School, a recently modernised 'federated' school on the south side of St Mary's. The kids are mostly fair-haired and unnaturally quiet. Students from the 'off islands' board in a hostel during the week rather than attempt the complicated, expensive and sometime dangerous (and sometimes impossible, given the tide) boat trip from their family homes and back every day. To study beyond GCSE they'll have to leave the Scillies, but many of them will return eventually, islanders at heart, only at home in a place whose population is smaller than the Yorkshire village where I grew up and which will soon receive its first traffic light, though only a temporary one, installed as a traffic-calming measure. As a further indication of the size of the place, I hear one teacher in the staff room saying to another, 'I'm going to walk up to the airport at lunchtime – I think I left my bike there.' The school-crossing attendant at Five Islands School must have one of the least stressful jobs in the world; there isn't a single vehicle or even a parent at the gates at the end of the school day as he directs all the kids out into the country lane, many of them on bikes. On the other side of that lane is an empty beach which I follow around the corner to the church. I'm looking for the Right Honourable the Lord Wilson of Rievaulx, aka Harold Wilson, Huddersfield's most famous son. His grave here makes a neat bookend for my journey, its counterpart being the statue of the former Labour prime minister in St George's Square outside Huddersfield railway station, which catches Wilson mid-stride in a baggy suit and with a purposeful air. His widow, the occasional poet Mary, stipulated that the statue shouldn't caricature her husband by depicting him with his trademark pipe, though his hand appears to be hiding something inside his right trouser pocket, which makes me wonder if pipe smoking and its concealment was part of the syllabus at Royds Hall School, where Wilson was educated. My dad, also a devoted pipe smoker who went to the same school, would often strike an identical pose, closing his fist over the smouldering bowl then stuffing it into his pocket while making a half-turn to the side to conduct a conversation. Waiting for a client one day in the concourse of Tameside Magistrates' Court during his time as a probation officer he was unexpectedly called in to give evidence. Midway through, the clerk halted proceedings to say, 'Excuse me, Mr Armitage, but you appear to be on fire.'

A bookend and a counterpart, then, but also a contrast, between the seventy thousand pounds' worth of bronze immortalising Wilson as the busy and important statesman marching between committee rooms and Cabinet meetings, and his resting place here, a metaphorical deckchair of grey granite and white pebbles facing the shore.

*

The boat that will ferry us across the sound between St Mary's and Tresco is called *Cyclone*. Is that a good name for a boat? It doesn't turn up but another does, this one called *Hurricane*. Is that better or worse? It's only a short skim over a strait of water never quite shallow enough for people of average height to walk but sometimes referred to as 'The Road'. On the quayside at New Grimsby we climb into a kind of articulated mini cattle train pulled by a tractor which drives along the harbour wall then steers inland, dropping off passengers and their luggage at various points around the circuit, depositing them at the doors of houses and holiday cottages called things like 'Lobster' and 'Snipe'. Our stop is the New Inn, which is pub, restaurant and hotel all rolled into one, run by manager Robin and owned by the Dorrien-Smith family, who preside over the Tresco Estate, which as far as I can tell is the whole island and everything on it.

The reading is in an hour but the only person in the bar so far is Slug, who has booked himself in and is nursing a pint in the corner. I don't have high hopes for the event. Everyone on these two square miles of land is a holidaymaker, or working for the holiday trade, and even though the start time has been brought forward in accordance with the tide, anyone sailing here from the other islands, not least St Mary's, where most of the human beings are, still risks being marooned for the night. Is poetry worth it? I go to the bedroom to prepare a set list and to try and shake some of the creases out of a clean shirt, thinking that coming here was a step too far, that I should have anticipated a diminuendo of interest across this petering archipelago and bowed out on the mainland, as a landlubber, where I belong. Can I really go through with it if the audience is just Sue looking at her feet, Slug looking at me through the cyclopean eye of the bottom of a pint pot, and

Robin refilling the optics behind the bar? When I come back downstairs, though, the public lounge is packed. Somehow, and from somewhere, people have turned up, so many people that I don't even bother counting them, just content myself that every alcove looks full and every seat appears taken. Even the pool table has been pushed to one side to create a bit more space. I use the long wooden key fob from my room as a gavel, banging on the side of a wooden stool to open proceedings, then for about an hour read poems of the sea, of the beach, of desert islands and stretches of water, of drownings and voyages, of shells and storms, imagined poems of pearl diving with mermaids and sailing around the world single-handedly in a terraced house, and the true story of the piece of coral found growing in my dad's ear. But finish with a poem of home, about a village on a hill, with only land beyond it in every direction, and beyond that more land, and still more land beyond. The questions at the end are fittingly strange, appropriately unreal.

'Do you write your own poems?' one woman wants to know. Everybody laughs.

A man in one of the booths asks, 'Is it true you're hoping to walk to Bryher then to Samson tomorrow?'

'Yes. Is it possible?'

'Only if you're Jesus.'

More laughter.

Finally, a woman at the back enquires if she can come to the front and read some of my work.

'I don't know if that's a good idea,' I say.

'I'll be good at it. I'm an auctioneer,' she replies.

On another day, in a hall or classroom or cafe or public house back along the northern fringe of the South West

Coast Path, I might have said yes. But this is the last reading, and the last word will be mine, so I say no. 'No,' I say.
And everybody cheers.

*

Even if the Scillies fall under the governance of the UK and
form part of the wider county of Cornwall and pay tax and
tribute to their royal freeholder, Prince Charles, there's a
feeling of emotional and political autonomy here, an atmosphere which the visitor tunes into pretty quickly. The five
main islands have their own status and their own reputa-
tions. If St Mary's is the polis, dominant in every way and
through every statistic, then St Martin's is its provincial elsewhere, and St Agnes its enigmatic alternative, and Bryher a
kind of people's republic looking sarcastically east across the
narrow channel towards Tresco, thought of by some as
affected and synthetic, offering a form of stage-managed
tourism and time-share heritage, though in reality Tresco is
too varied to be so casually stereotyped and easily characterised. The beaches on its west coast, beyond the dunes, are
genuinely and naturally beautiful, not to mention eye-
wateringly bright when the sun ricochets off the white pebbles and platinum-coloured sand. And the north-west end
of the island is rough heath becoming virtual moorland
towards its furthest hill, capped with the tumbledown
remains of an old castle. The south and central area is almost
subtropical by comparison, and more cultivated in every
respect, both around the Abbey Gardens and the toy-town
holiday village with its block-paved 'streets' and contemporary cottages. Electric buggies are parked up outside some

of the dwellings, a concession to the infirm and the down-right lazy on an island where proper vehicles are the privilege of the worker. It's dark, and we've walked past the Great Pool, a long freshwater lagoon flanked by a million reeds whose long shafts stand like the tall spears of a resting army. An owl screeches, waders pipe and flute in the blackness, unnamed creatures in the boggy undergrowth send thick, oily ripples out across the water. The spilt mercury of the moon's reflection extends from the head of the lake right to our feet. On the opposite side of the island, around Old Grimsby Harbour, moonlight sheens off the mudflats and picks out rocky protuberances in the bay, some like the hulks of scuttled ships, one particular silhouette like a black submarine just breaking the surface, complete with conning tower and gun emplacement. It's a reminder that in reality the Scillies are actually hundreds, perhaps thousands of islands and islets, some which sustain life and host viable human communities, others which appear and disappear with the tide and have come and gone over millions of years through changes in sea level and movements of sandbars, silt and reefs. White Island, St Helen's, Northwethel and Tean are all out there beyond this shore, plus dozens and dozens of smaller islands, each with their own off-islands and archipelagos, a descending scale of geographies and categories in which a single outcrop, lone rock or even a boulder might still be deserving of its own name and place on the map. The darkness grows darker, and it's late now, inasmuch as 11 p.m. on the Scillies feels like the equivalent of 2 a.m. back home. The quietness is the kind that reduces a conversation to whispers, and we haven't seen another person for well over an hour. From a vantage point on the way back to the New Inn I can see what I take to be Samson, object of tomorrow's fording and my final destination, the island I have deemed the most walkable westerly terminus on this particular vector, with its two summits and the cleavage which separates them just about visible against the last glow of dusk on the western horizon. There appears to be a light on the island, a tiny orange pinprick pulsing on and off, Samson's incorporeal single resident perhaps, though it could just as easily be a marker buoy out in the sound, or even a lantern tied to a donkey's tail, designed to lure the naïve and unwary traveller onto the rocks.

Tresco to Bryher, Bryher to Samson

Thursday 19 September

To be here at the lowest possible low Autumn tide I've orchestrated my arrival on the Scillies to coincide with a full moon, though all the lunar phase calendars I've consulted suggest peak gravitational pull could occur at any time between 10.30 a.m. and well after noon. Barometric pressure also plays a role in tidal extent, every added millibar (or hectopascal in new money) displacing sea level by one centimetre in a scientifically perfect world, as the weight of the atmosphere effectively bears down on the surface of the water. The higher the pressure, the lower the low tide, and on that basis the omens are not good: it's a damp, drizzly morning when I pull back the curtains at about half past eight, a wet breeze mussing the hair of a palm tree outside the window and an awful lot of brine between here and Bryher. Samson is just a Rothko-like smear in the distance.

The New Inn offers its guests free use of Wellington boots, and there are a dozen or so pairs to choose from by the door to the beer garden. 'You'll need waders where you're going,' says one man as he squeezes past. His friend chips in with, 'Or a diving bell.' Several people have suggested Plum Island as the most feasible point of departure, a conical layer cake of matter at the far end of the bay, fringed by black-green seaweed around its pedestal, followed by concentric rings of rust, then orange, then yellow, then white rocks, with a tuft of vegetation on its crown, and resting on that a walrus-shaped boulder with its nose pointing to the south. Or am I looking at Merrick Island, at the northern end of a sandbar in the sound? The shape and pattern of the islands seem to change all the time, morphing and moving with alterations in weather and light and tide, an evolving and unreliable flux of land and water, islands being born and buried twice a day, a geography difficult to fathom or to trust.

Eight or nine of us have set out along the road from the New Inn, and are joined by seven or eight others, people stepping out of cottage doorways or coming over the hill or wandering up the beach, all making for Plum Island, which now that the sea has begun to drain away is not an island but a mini headland connected to the shore by a thin spine, like a newel ball at the end of a banister rail. A blackbird on the top bar of a gate lets me walk within touching distance before it hops onto the wall and takes up its singing again. There are people here from yesterday's reading, including Do You Write Your Own Poems lady, the Auctioneer, an American man who sat behind us in the dining room last night attempting to order an infinitesimally detailed meal of highly specific provenance, limited calorific value and negligible fat content (he had the profiteroles for pudding), plus a woman who fell over us on the stairs going up to bed, saying, 'I'm very drunk,' followed by her husband, who nodded and grinned. They're all here. One elderly man suddenly emerges from the waves, his wetsuit darkened by immersion to well above his midriff, inviting us to follow him back into the water because he *knows the way*. Other voices are suggesting a slight curving detour to the south, or

waiting another half an hour, and several hands are pointing at numerous natural 'causeways' (i.e. mirages and opti-
cal illusions) just beneath the surface that might offer a safe
passage to Bryher, whose coast is no more than two or three
hundred yards away but beyond a stretch of sea whose
depth, direction and mood are impossible to judge. In the
end I decide on the most direct route, the most immediate
action, and just go walking forward. I *walk into space*. Others follow, some directly behind, some sticking to their
arcane mental maps of these waters and their chosen course,
maybe twenty of us in all easing our way into the shallow
flow, slopping and splashing towards the far shore. Occasionally my foot disappears into soft mud or down a rut on
the seabed, but it's hardly an abyss, and nowhere on the
crossing is deeper than eighteen inches at most, more like a
wide and gentle river than part of the North Atlantic. A red
starfish lies on the bottom, beneath the unsteady haze of the
clear water, almost as red as the trousers and hat of Michael
Morpurgo, who has put down his pen, put aside his story
and walked down through the garden of his rented writing
retreat to welcome us ashore. He's a summer migrant here,
and like many writers and artists who thrive on the slow,
uninterrupted pace of the Scillies he has incorporated this
particular island into his working practice and his creative
mindset for many years. Beyond the slippery, stony foreshore we pick up a grassy path that skirts the southern nose
of Bryher. Leaving the path we push through tall ferns, then
out onto a bald knoll where large boulders of ivory-coloured
granite have shouldered out of the earth, to where the view
opens up and Samson stands directly in front, North Hill
the nearer, with the summit of the slightly higher South

Hill just visible over its shoulder, vague traces of walls and old fields discernible on its flanks, and the rocky tongue of Ballard Point reaching towards us. But between here and there stands a body of water which is truly the sea, a channel of waves and currents, not in any way the preserve of the humble pedestrian or even the competent swimmer but the domain of the oarsmen and the craft, a barrier of formidable and unfordable water lying transverse across the path, with Samson on the far shore, unattainable and removed, and me on this shore with a newly written, folded-up poem in my pocket and my two feet stopped in their tracks, pointing south, at the water's edge. It's the end of the road.

Scillonia

The locals move the hills around at night.
A stone armada moors in the harbour at low tide.
Sleep with an open hand and a dunnock
nests in the palm, raises its young.
Lord Harold lounges in his beachside grave,
eye sockets full of the west, pink sea thrift
crowning his skull, an acetylene wand
of purple agapanthus in his fossil fist.
This crossroads shrine is in fact a shop:
a bowl of eggs, six carrots, an honesty box.
Looking down, the stars see constellations
in the firmament of beacons and buoys.
Samson's castaway snuffs out his hurricane lamp
then slides in his tomb. Along the verge,
a dozen blonde narcissi are walking to school.

Reckoning Up

I won't be doing any more long walks. This walk was conceived as unfinished business, chosen as a direct alternative and a determined, symmetrical opposite to the Pennine Way, and that business is now concluded. As well as describing differences in geography and landscape, the mischief-maker in me had it in mind to compare the generosity of the people of the north with those of the south, and to compare my poetic standing in the two regions based on the contents of the sock, as measured in pounds and pence. But as the days went by that notion began to fade, or the crudeness of it started to dawn on me. In the end I didn't even count the takings, just dipped into the stash whenever I needed to and settled a credit-card bill for rail fares, steam-train rides and taxis on the way down, for planes, trains and automobiles on the way home, and for clothing and gear bought in advance, including one very expensive hat. In the end I was left with little to call a wage of any kind but enough to have existed happily and healthily for the duration of the trip and to have paid my way and proved a couple of points, one about being able to live on my wits and my feet for three weeks in an unfamiliar part of the world, and another regarding the vitality of poetry and people's ongoing interest in it, whatever its contemporary reputation. I won't say that I've hung up my boots altogether, but the new ones are still lying snug in their tissue-lined box like a pair of new-born puppies, and as far as I know the old ones are still parked in the tack room of a house in Cape Cornwall, decomposing.

*

It was frustrating not to finish, but walking to Samson was always something of a poetic fantasy based on unsubstantiated rumours and casual research. People are still adamant that it's possible to make the crossing from the southern tip of Bryher on foot at very specific times of the year during very particular weather conditions, but I've failed to reach destinations before, sometimes deliberately so, and I'm persuaded by the idea that there should always be a Samson or an Edale up ahead, some desirable but unreachable place on the horizon, beyond a dangerous current or a storm-lashed hill, somewhere out of range. Remembering my dad's remark about Moses I suppose I could have lifted my staff and attempted to part the waves with a grand biblical gesture. Or I could have lowered it into the water and pushed it out to sea, offering that time-honed and much-travelled limb of Yorkshire holly to the waves, launching the stick which had walked with me from beginning to end, turning it over to the mercy of the elements and the unpredictable currents of the Atlantic as I'd always meant to. But my stick wasn't there, and hadn't been with me for over a week. When last seen it was leaning against a car-park wall in Newquay and I didn't register its absence until after the Gannel and halfway across Crantock Beach, by which time I'd gone too far to turn back. I phoned Jon at the Cafe Irie, who made a sweep of the neighbouring streets and put their 'specials' blackboard out on the street with a chalked appeal for the lost item. Well-wishers and sympathisers tweeted and blogged about it, and those who know about these things told me that social media was 'buzzing' with the story of the missing stick, to the point where it had its own internet trolls and a man in Idaho was claiming to have found it in a dried-up creek on his ranch. But the stick had gone. Left in one of the most mundane and inauspicious locations on the whole expedition and never seen since. By that stage it was a finely tuned instrument, the innocent green bark having weathered to a mature dark brown, its hoof hardened by impact against stone, cured by seawater and scoured to a pearly smoothness by sand, and the handle smoothed by human touch and sweaty palms to an ergonomically pleasing texture and shape. I'd like to think it found its way into the hands of another walker and is being put to the use for which it was originally whittled, and that right now it might be clomping along a stretch of the Coast Path or assisting a trekker through some more exotic and adventurous location, the jungles of Papua New Guinea maybe, or across the Nazca Plain. Or I could think of it as my final barter, a trade for the 260 miles and three weeks of literal and metaphorical beachcombing, one loyal and trusty stick with one ultimately careless owner in exchange for all the lists and roll calls. For all the products in a haberdasher's store; all the colours of sand and the washed-up objects on a Devon beach; all the pots and pans and pencils and pens in a mothballed studio cabin overlooking the sea; all the trophies and mementoes decorating a harbourmaster's cottage; all the grisly relics and occult books in a museum of witchcraft; all

the squabbling finches and tits on a bird-feeder in a Cornish
garden after rain; and for the inventory of items and objects
that found their way into a poet's sock: a raffle ticket, a
bookie's pencil, a packet of crumbs that was once a biscuit, a
tube of Smarties, one packet of disposable Magic Towels,
one 140g packet of Bon Bon wine gums, a set of six postcards showing views of North Devon and Exmoor, a book
of six first-class stamps, one plastic badger, a handwritten,
alphabetically ordered list of international goalkeepers, one
feather (juvenile herring gull?), five McDonald's vouchers
for meal deals comprising a regular burger and a medium
drink, one CAMRA membership application form, two
bookmarks from a bookshop in Crediton, one copy of
Resurgence & Ecologist magazine, the 7 September issue of
New Musical Express featuring Arctic Monkeys' new album
AM, one Twinings cranberry-and-raspberry-infusion tea-
bag, one tube of contact-lens cleaning solution, one lemon-
scented moisturised hand-wipe in a partly opened foil
wrapper, a small white pebble, numerous seashells, one
Thai Airways duty-free plastic bag, four interlocking plastic hearts, one folded paper 'wishmaker', one copy of Seamus Heaney's *Human Chain* signed by the author, two
'pamper parlour' vouchers for Budock Water Village Hall,
one small black button, one big green button, one Atlantic
Brewery beer-pump label, one Brazilian banknote folded
into the shape of a starfish or futuristic spaceship, one 'I'm
an Avenger' lick 'n' stick transfer, one packet of unidenti-
fied seeds, one small packet of Tesco's own brand raisins,
one Dr Munzinger strawberry-flavoured wafer bar, one
Viagra-endorsed pocket knife and key fob, two pairs of
pure lambswool walking socks, one box of Yorkshire Tea,

one 125g bar of Lindt milk chocolate, one sprig of pine, one
'How To Speak Cornish' leaflet, one business card with the
offer of a complimentary dinner at the Halestown Inn, one
10cl bottle of strawberry-and-cream-flavoured Cornish
Lust liqueur, two toffees, one 5ml bottle of Glenlivet whisky, one 5p fuel coupon for use at any BP garage, one tube of
wooden toothpicks, one purple ribbon, one safety pin, one
bullet, one German condom and a hard-boiled egg.

Acknowledgements

I would like to acknowledge my indebtedness to Caroline Hawkridge for managing and steering this adventure from well ahead of the starting line to well beyond the finishing post. Without her creative intelligence, organisational aptitude and enduring patience the walk would never have evolved beyond a dotted line along several unwieldy maps. For joining those dots, and for her tact, guile, warmth, humour and spreadsheets, I am sincerely grateful.

I would also like to thank the following people for being curious and kind enough to welcome an itinerant poet into their lives for a few hours in the late summer of 2013, for being hosts, organisers, guides, sherpas, photographers and bloggers and for keeping me company from the gates of Butlins to the coast of Bryher: Emma Kelly, Operations Assistant, Butlins; Jill Walmsley; Suki Lilienthal, Sandra Sidaway and the Friends of Coleridge Cottage; Caroline Taylor, Jane Honess, Stephen Hayes and the National Trust, Coleridge Cottage; the West Somerset College's Subject Leader for Hospitality Adrian Fleming and partner Becky; staff and students of The Combe restaurant; colleagues Hannah Donnellan and Candice Dean; Phoebe Stukes and family; John and Kate Dee and friends; Tim Dee; Wanda Tait; missing journalist Martin Hesp; Mark Radcliffe and Stuart Maconie; John and Linda Oliver, Tilla Brading and

Porlock Arts Festival; Derek Wolfe – great to see you again, Derek; Margaret Drabble for morning coffee; Anna Toeman; Annie Coombs and Chris Driver; Andy and Sue North at Southcliffe B&B and Queenie, the best-dressed dog in town; Carolynn Gold and friends at Barbrook Village Hall Trust; Rob Schofield; Roland Keith and John the cyclist; Penny and John at Mellstock House B&B, plus poet-spotters; Pat Chesterton and volunteers at Combe Martin Museum; Alison Heimann, Community Engagement and Communications, North Devon Coast AONB; Adrian Moss at Woolacombe Bay Hotel; 'Tall' Paul Trueman, Heather Pritchard and Georgeham Village Hall; North Devon Coast AONB ranger Dave Edgecombe; Braunton Library for advice about (the non-existence of) local cobblers; Geoffrey and Kirsty Everett-Brown and family and friends at Heavenly House; David Job, Simeon Day, Charlie, Hern and Orla at Yarde Orchard Bunkhouse; Richard Wolfenden-Brown, Director, and staff at the Plough Arts Centre; Gill Clayton; Simon Milward; Des and Clare; Ian and Gerald; Andrew Moorhouse; Fiona and Oliver Chope and family, and all at Walter Henry's bookshop; Justin Seedhouse, National Trust; Joy James and Clovelly harbour master Stephen Perham; the Hon. John Rous, squire of Clovelly; Sue Haworth, Events Organiser, Clovelly Estate; Sally Stevens, Manager, the Red Lion; Elle Jarvis, Susan Schmarsel; Sir Hugh and Lady Angela Stucley at Hartland Abbey with Alison and Andrew Heimann, and party helpers Scott, Ellen, Louisa and friends; Gigha Klinkenborg, North Devon Coast AONB; Kevin and Lesley Duff; Amy Sands; Bob and Yvonne Moore and Grant; Rod Landman, Lou Griffiths and sons; Mark and Pene North, Peter and

Acknowledgements

Janice North; Bryony and Andrew; Dorigen and Tony Couchman; Kate Gamm, Director, Calstock Arts; James Crowden and Carla; Jan and Jackie; Claire and Ben Barratt and family, and dog Sprockett and fellow diners; Graham King at the Museum of Witchcraft, Boscastle; Brenda Nagy, Manager, Boscastle YHA, and driver Alison; Janey Coomber, Ellen Hawley and friends from Just Desserts and North Cornwall Poetry Stanza; Max Burrows; Frankie and Ray; Tom Scott and family; Penelope Shuttle and Falmouth Poetry Group; Ron Johns; bartenders Jane Finlay, Camilla Whitehill and Michael; 'Frank Sinatra'; Merryn Kent, Reader Services Officer, Cornwall Council, and Mike Kent, and daughter Kerris; 'Frank Sinatra'; Sue Pinch and colleagues at Wadebridge Library; Stuart and Sarah Thomson and family and friends at Atlantic Brewery; life-guard Rosie; Jane Darke; Richard Evans, Terry and Marianne Evans; Jon Evison and team at Cafe Irie; Joe Morris; Jo 'Josie Ghost' Horsey; sand artist Tony Plant; Sara Black and friends; Charles; Colonel Cornelius; Peter and Rufus; searchers of the lost stick; Fern Pit Cafe for advice on the Gannel's tides; Slug; Ben Job at Schooner's Bistro; Diana Bushe at the Malthouse B&B; Richard and Julie Wadman; David Durham, Dee Bray and Claire Pearce at Porthminster Gallery; St Ives September Festival; Anna Selvey and students Jacob, Chris, Jack, Scott, Alice, Ellie, Lucy, Kendall, Mary, Tesni and Sally from Truro High School; Mav, Emma, Penny and Fred and friends at the Celtic Roundhouse, Bodrifty; Michael and Jane Adams; Jane Weller; Charles Inkin, The Gurnard's Head; Tara and Mark Physick and family; Henry Garfit, founder, Newlyn School of Art; Mark Spray, artist and tutor, Newlyn School

Acknowledgements

of Art; Jesse Leroy-Smith, and everyone who swabbed out the old fish processing factory and contributed to the 'Suspended Sentences' exhibition; Bev Knox at Five Islands School, St Mary's; Lucy Dorrien-Smith, Tresco Estate, and colleagues Alasdair Moore, Jackie Hughes; Robin Lawson, Manager, New Inn, Tresco Island Office and Bryher Boats for advice about tides and boat services; Helen and David Constantine; Michael and Clare Morpurgo; Angela and David White. And, as always, to the hooded lady who propositioned me on the path between Clovelly and Hartland Quay.

Also by Simon Armitage

Walking Home

One summer, Simon Armitage decided to walk the Pennine Way – a challenging 256-mile route usually approached from south to north, with the sun, wind and rain at your back. However, he resolved to tackle it back to front, walking home towards the Yorkshire village where he was born, travelling as a 'modern troubadour', without a penny in his pocket and singing for his supper with poetry readings in village halls, churches, pubs and living rooms. *Walking Home* describes his extraordinary, yet ordinary, journey of human endeavour, unexpected kindnesses and terrible blisters.

'So observant, so funny and so intensely likeable you leave it wishing he's picked a longer route.' *Telegraph*

'Armitage makes an agreeably droll travel writer . . . His affectionate tale on the English at play is truly Betjemanesque.' *Sunday Times*

'*Walking Home* is a charming account of Armitage's epic journey, brought to life by the quirky characters he meets along the way . . . a fun and engaging piece of travel writing.' *Time Out*

ff

Faber & Faber – a home for writers

Faber & Faber is one of the great independent publishing houses in London. We were established in 1929 by Geoffrey Faber and our first editor was T. S. Eliot. We are proud to publish prize-winning fiction and non-fiction, as well as an unrivalled list of modern poets and playwrights. Among our list of writers we have five Booker Prize winners and eleven Nobel Laureates, and we continue to seek out the most exciting and innovative writers at work today.

www.faber.co.uk – a home for readers

The Faber website is the place where you can find all the latest news on our writers and events, and browse and buy in the Faber shop. You can also join the free Faber Members programme for discounts, exclusive access to events and our range of hand-bound Collectors' Editions.